Informing the legislative debate since 1914

Arms Control and Nonproliferation: A Catalog of Treaties and Agreements

Amy F. Woolf
Specialist in Nuclear Weapons Policy

Paul K. Kerr
Analyst in Nonproliferation

Mary Beth D. Nikitin
Specialist in Nonproliferation

July 21, 2014

Congressional Research Service

7-5700

www.crs.gov

RL33865

Summary

Arms control and nonproliferation efforts are two of the tools that have occasionally been used to implement U.S. national security strategy. Although some believe these tools do little to restrain the behavior of U.S. adversaries, while doing too much to restrain U.S. military forces and operations, many other analysts see them as an effective means to promote transparency, ease military planning, limit forces, and protect against uncertainty and surprise. Arms control and nonproliferation efforts have produced formal treaties and agreements, informal arrangements, and cooperative threat reduction and monitoring mechanisms. The pace of implementation for many of these agreements slowed during the Clinton Administration, and the Bush Administration usually preferred unilateral or ad hoc measures to formal treaties and agreements to address U.S. security concerns. But the Obama Administration resumed bilateral negotiations with Russia and pledged its support for a number of multilateral arms control and nonproliferation efforts.

The United States and Soviet Union began to sign agreements limiting their strategic offensive nuclear weapons in the early 1970s. Progress in negotiating and implementing these agreements was often slow, and subject to the tenor of the broader U.S.-Soviet relationship. As the Cold War drew to a close in the late 1980s, the pace of negotiations quickened, with the two sides signing treaties limiting intermediate range and long-range weapons. But progress again slowed in the 1990s, as U.S. missile defense plans and a range of other policy conflicts intervened in the U.S.-Russian relationship. At the same time, however, the two sides began to cooperate on securing and eliminating Soviet-era nuclear, chemical, and biological weapons. Through these efforts, the United States allocates more than $1 billion each year to threat reduction programs in the former Soviet Union. However, these programs may slow or stall in the next few years.

The United States is also a prominent actor in an international regime that attempts to limit the spread of nuclear weapons. This regime, although suffering from some setbacks in recent years in Iran and North Korea, includes formal treaties, export control coordination and enforcement, U.N. resolutions, and organizational controls. The Nuclear Nonproliferation Treaty (NPT) serves as the cornerstone of this regime, with all but four nations participating in it. The International Atomic Energy Agency not only monitors nuclear programs to make sure they remain peaceful, but also helps nations develop and advance those programs. Other measures, such as sanctions, interdiction efforts, and informal cooperative endeavors, also seek to slow or stop the spread of nuclear materials and weapons.

The international community has also adopted a number of agreements that address non-nuclear weapons. The CFE Treaty and Open Skies Treaty sought to stabilize the conventional balance in Europe in the waning years of the Cold War. Other arrangements seek to slow the spread of technologies that nations could use to develop advanced conventional weapons. The Chemical Weapons and Biological Weapons Conventions sought to eliminate both of these types of weapons completely.

This report will be updated annually or as needed.

Contents

Tables

Appendixes

Contacts

Introduction

National Security, Arms Control, and Nonproliferation

For much of the past century, U.S. national security strategy focused on several core, interrelated objectives. These include enhancing U.S. security at home and abroad; promoting U.S. economic prosperity; and promoting free markets and democracy around the world. The United States has used both unilateral and multilateral mechanisms to achieve these objectives, with varying amounts of emphasis at different times. These mechanisms have included a range of military, diplomatic, and economic tools.

One of these core objectives—enhancing U.S. security—generally is interpreted as the effort to protect the nation's interests and includes, for instance, protecting the lives and safety of Americans; maintaining U.S. sovereignty over its values, territory, and institutions; and promoting the nation's well-being. The United States has wielded a deep and wide range of military, diplomatic, and economic tools to protect and advance its security interests. These include, for instance, the deployment of military forces to deter, dissuade, persuade, or compel others; the formation of alliances and coalitions to advance U.S. interests and counter aggression; and the use of U.S. economic power to advance its agenda or promote democratization, or to impose sanctions or withhold U.S. economic support to condemn or punish states hostile to U.S. interests.

In this context, arms control and nonproliferation efforts are two of the tools that have occasionally been used to implement the U.S. national security strategy. They generally are not pursued as ends in and of themselves, and many argue that they should not become more important than the strategy behind them. But many believe their effective employment can be critical to the success of that broader strategy. Many analysts see them as a complement to, rather than a substitute for, military or economic efforts.

Effective arms control measures are thought to enhance U.S. national security in a number of ways. For example, arms control measures that promote transparency might increase U.S. knowledge about and understanding of the size, make-up, and operations of an opposing military force. This might not only ease U.S. military planning, but it might also reduce an opponent's incentives for and opportunities to attack U.S. forces, or the forces of its friends and allies. Transparency measures can also build confidence among wary adversaries. Effective arms control measures can also be designed to complement U.S. force structure objectives by limiting or restraining U.S. and other nations' forces. In an era of declining defense budget resources, arms control measures may also help ensure reciprocity in force reductions. Indeed, some analysts consider such arms control measures essential to the success of our national military objectives.

Similarly, U.S. officials from several Administrations have identified efforts to prevent the further spread of weapons of mass destruction and their means of delivery to be an essential element of U.S. national security. For one reason, proliferation can exacerbate regional tensions that might escalate to conflict and involve or threaten U.S. forces or those of its friends and allies. Proliferation might also introduce new and unexpected threats to the U.S. homeland. Furthermore, proliferation can greatly complicate U.S. national military strategy, force structure design, and conduct of operations. And these weapons could pose a threat to the U.S. homeland if they were acquired by terrorists or subnational groups. Hence, the United States employs diplomatic, economic, and military tools to restrain these threats and enhance its national security.

During the Cold War, arms control played a key role in the relationship between the United States and Soviet Union. Although the agreements rarely forced either side to accept significant changes in its planned nuclear forces, the arms control process, and the formal negotiations, were often one of the few channels for communication between the United States and Soviet Union. Further, the United States participated in many multilateral regimes that sought to limit the spread of nuclear, chemical, and biological weapons and their means of delivery. Since the 1990s, it has also extended assistance to Russia, and other former Soviet states, in an effort to reduce the threat that these weapons might fall into the hands of hostile states or non-state actors. It is now exploring the possible use of these tools to provide other nations with assistance in containing and controlling weapons and weapons-grade materials.

During the George W. Bush Administration, the President and many in his Administration questioned the degree to which arms control negotiations and formal treaties could enhance U.S. security objectives. They argued that the United States did not need formal treaties to reduce or restrain its strategic nuclear forces. As a result, President Bush initially intended to reduce U.S. nuclear forces without signing a treaty that would require Russia to do the same. The Bush Administration only incorporated these reductions into a formal treaty after Russia insisted on such a document. Similarly, some in the Bush Administration argued that some formal, multilateral arms control regimes went too far in restraining U.S. options without limiting the forces of potential adversaries. Instead, the Administration preferred, when necessary, that the United States take unilateral military action or join in ad hoc coalitions to stem the proliferation of weapons of mass destruction.

The Obama Administration has altered this approach, and has sought to enhance the role of arms control and nonproliferation agreements in U.S. national security policy. In a speech in Prague in April 2009, the President outlined an agenda that included the pursuit of a new strategic arms control treaty with Russia, efforts to secure the ratification and entry into force of the Comprehensive Test Ban Treaty, and the eventual negotiation of a Fissile Material Control Treaty. President Obama also convened an international nuclear security summit, in April 2010, in an effort to win global cooperation in efforts to contain and eliminate vulnerable nuclear materials. The President also pledged to take a number of steps to strengthen the Nuclear Nonproliferation Treaty in conjunction with its review conference in May 2010.[1]

The absence of confidence in arms control during the George W. Bush Administration extended to the State Department, where the Administration removed the phrase "arms control" from all bureaus that were responsible for this policy area. The focus remained on nonproliferation, but it was seen as a policy area that no longer required formal treaties to meet its objectives. This, too, changed with the Obama Administration. The State Department has restored the phrase "arms control" to some bureau titles, and "arms control" is again listed as a central issue on the State Department website.[2]

President Obama's embrace of arms control and nonproliferation tools to address U.S. national security needs led many to expect wide-ranging agreements and activities in pursuit of these goals. However, efforts on this agenda produced limited results during President Obama's first term. The United States and Russia signed the 2010 New START Treaty, and have begun to implement its modest reductions, but there is little evidence of progress toward discussions on

---

[1] http://www.whitehouse.gov/the_press_office/Remarks-By-President-Barack-Obama-In-Prague-As-Delivered/.

[2] http://www.state.gov/.

further reductions on nuclear weapons. The President has not yet sought Senate advice and consent on the Comprehensive Test Ban Treaty, while the Fissile Material Control Treaty remains stalled in the U.N. Conference on Disarmament. Moreover, critics note that the Administration has yet to find a formula to stop either North Korea's pursuit of nuclear weapons or Iran's nuclear program, which leaves key nonproliferation goals unmet. As a result, many have questioned how well these tools will serve U.S. national security interests over the next few years.

The Arms Control Agenda

The United States has participated in numerous arms control and nonproliferation efforts over the past 40 years. These efforts have produced formal treaties and agreements that impose restrictions on U.S. military forces and activities, informal arrangements and guidelines that the United States has agreed to observe, and unilateral restraints on military forces and activities that the United States has adopted either on its own, or in conjunction with reciprocal restraints on other nations' forces and activities. Because these arms control arrangements affect U.S. national security, military programs, force levels, and defense spending, Congress has shown a continuing interest in the implementation of existing agreements and ongoing negotiations.

The changing international environment in the 1990s led many analysts to believe that the United States and other nations could enter a new era of restraint in weapons deployments, weapons transfers, and military operations. These hopes were codified in several treaties signed between 1991 and 1996, such as the Strategic Arms Reduction Treaties (START I and START II), the Chemical Weapons Convention, and the Comprehensive Nuclear Test Ban Treaty. Yet, for many, hopes for a new era were clouded by the slow pace of ratification and implementation for many agreements. The 1991 START I Treaty did not enter into force until late 1994; the 1993 START II Treaty never entered into force and was replaced by a new, less detailed Strategic Offensive Reductions Treaty in 2002. The 1996 Comprehensive Test Ban Treaty (CTBT), in spite of widespread international support, failed to win approval from the U.S. Senate in October 1999. Furthermore, India, Pakistan, Iran, and North Korea raised new questions about the viability of the Nuclear Nonproliferation Treaty and its role in stemming nuclear proliferation.

Some progress did occur in the latter years of the decade. In 1997, the United States and Russia, the two nations with the largest stockpiles of chemical weapons, both ratified the Chemical Weapons Convention. In December 1997, more than 120 nations signed an international agreement banning the use of anti-personnel land mines; however, a number of major nations, including the United States, have so far declined to sign. However, the U.S. Senate's rejection of the CTBT, the Bush Administration's withdrawal from the ABM Treaty in 2002, and the U.S. rejection of a verification protocol for the Biological Weapons Convention led many nations to question the U.S. commitment to the arms control process.

During the Bush Administration, the United States outlined new initiatives in nonproliferation policy that took a far less formal approach, with voluntary guidelines and voluntary participation replacing treaties and multilateral conventions. The Bush Administration also signaled a change in the focus of U.S. nonproliferation policy. Instead of offering its support to international regimes that sought to establish nonproliferation norms that apply to all nations, the Bush Administration turned to arrangements that sought, instead, to prevent proliferation only to those nations and groups that the United States believed could threaten U.S. or international security. In essence, nonproliferation became a tool of anti-terrorism policy.

The Obama Administration also views nonproliferation policy as a tool of anti-terrorism policy, and has highlighted the importance of keeping nuclear, chemical, and biological weapons away from non-state actors who might threaten the United States or its allies. But it also views nonproliferation as a more general tool of U.S. national security policy. And, where the Bush Administration focused its efforts on denying these weapons to specific nations or groups who might threaten the United States, the Obama Administration has adopted the more general goals of establishing and supporting international norms and regimes to control these weapons, regardless of which nations might seek them. For example, in a speech in Moscow in July 2009, President Obama noted that "the notion that prestige comes from holding these weapons, or that we can protect ourselves by picking and choosing which nations can have these weapons, is an illusion." He went on to state that stopping the spread of nuclear weapons "is not about singling out individual nations—it's about the responsibilities of all nations."[3]

This report provides an overview of many of the key arms control and nonproliferation agreements and endeavors of the past 40 years. It is divided into three sections. The first describes arms control efforts between the United States and the states of the former Soviet Union, covering both formal, bilateral treaties, and the cooperative threat reduction process. The second section describes multilateral nuclear nonproliferation efforts, covering both formal treaties and less formal accommodations that have been initiated in recent years. The final section reviews treaties and agreements that address chemical, biological, and conventional weapons.

The report concludes with several appendices. These provide a list of treaties and agreements that the United States is a party to, a description of the treaty ratification process, and a list of the bilateral and international organizations tasked with implementation of arms control efforts.

Arms Control Between the United States and States of the Former Soviet Union

The Early Years: SALT I and SALT II

The United States and Soviet Union signed their first formal agreements limiting nuclear offensive and defensive weapons in May 1972. The Strategic Arms Limitation Talks, known as SALT, produced two agreements—the *Interim Agreement ... on Certain Measures with Respect to the Limitation of Strategic Offensive Arms* and the *Treaty ... on the Limitation of Anti-Ballistic Missile Systems.* These were followed, in 1979, by the Strategic Arms Limitation Treaty, known as SALT II, which sought to codify equal limits on U.S. and Soviet strategic offensive nuclear forces.

The Interim Agreement on Offensive Arms

The Interim Agreement on Offensive Arms imposed a freeze on the number of launchers for intercontinental ballistic missiles (ICBMs) and submarine-launched ballistic missiles (SLBMs) that the United States and Soviet Union could deploy. The parties agreed that they would not begin construction of new ICBM launchers after July 1, 1972; at the time the United States had

---

[3] http://www.america.gov/st/texttrans-english/2009/July/20090707062839abretnuh3.549922e-02 html&distid=ucs.

1,054 ICBM launchers and the Soviet Union had 1,618 ICBM launchers. They also agreed to freeze their number of SLBM launchers and modern ballistic missile submarines, although they could add SLBM launchers if they retired old ICBM launchers. A protocol to the Treaty indicated that the United States could deploy up to 710 SLBM launchers on 44 submarines, and the Soviet Union could deploy up to 950 SLBM launchers on 62 submarines.

The inequality in these numbers raised serious concerns both in Congress and in the policy community in Washington. When approving the agreement, Congress adopted a provision, known as the Jackson amendment, that mandated that all future arms control agreements would have to contain equal limits for the United States and Soviet Union.

The Interim Agreement was to remain in force for five years, unless the parties replaced it with a more comprehensive agreement limiting strategic offensive weapons. In 1977, both nations agreed to observe the agreement until the completed the SALT II Treaty.

The Strategic Arms Limitation Treaty (SALT II)

The United States and Soviet Union completed the SALT II Treaty in June 1979, after seven years of negotiations. During these negotiations, the United States sought limits on quantitative and qualitative changes in Soviet forces. The U.S. negotiating position also reflected the congressional mandate for numerically equal limits on both nations' forces. As a result, the treaty limited each nation to a total of 2,400 ICBM launchers, SLBM launchers and heavy bombers, with this number declining to 2,250 by January 1, 1981. Within this total, the Treaty contained sublimits for the numbers launchers that could be deployed for ICBMs with multiple independent reentry vehicles (MIRVed ICBMs); MIRVed ICBMs and MIRVed SLBMs; and MIRVed ICBMs, MIRVed SLBMs, MIRVed air-to-surface ballistic missiles (ASBMs) and heavy bombers. The Treaty would not have limited the total number of warheads that could be carried on these delivery vehicles, which was a growing concern with the deployment of large numbers of multiple warhead missiles, but the nations did agree that they would not increase the numbers of warheads on existing types of missiles and would not test new types of ICBMs with more than 10 warheads and new types of SLBMs with more than 14 warheads. They also agreed to provisions that were designed to limit missile modernization programs, in an effort to restrain qualitative improvements in their strategic forces.

Although it contained equal limits on U.S. and Soviet forces, the SALT II Treaty still proved to be highly controversial. Some analysts argued that the Treaty would fail to curb the arms race because the limits on forces were equal to the numbers already deployed by the United States and Soviet Union; they argued for lower limits and actual reductions. Other analysts argued that the Treaty would allow the Soviet Union to maintain strategic superiority over the United States because the Soviet force of large, land-based ballistic missiles would be able to carry far greater numbers of warheads, even within the equal limits on delivery vehicles, than U.S. ballistic missiles. Some argued that, with this advantage, the Soviet Union would be able to target all U.S. land-based ICBMs in a first strike, which created a "window of vulnerability" for the United States. The Treaty's supporters argued that the Soviet advantage in large MIRVed ICBMs was more than offset by the U.S. advantage in SLBM warheads, which could not be destroyed in a first strike and could retaliate against Soviet targets, and the U.S. advantage in heavy bombers.

The continuing Soviet build-up of strategic nuclear forces, along with the taking of U.S. hostages in Iran and other challenges to the U.S. international position in the late 1970s, combined with the perceived weaknesses to the Treaty to raise questions about whether the Senate would muster the votes needed to consent to the Treaty's ratification. When the Soviet Union invaded Afghanistan in December 1979, President Carter withdrew the Treaty from the Senate's consideration.

The ABM Treaty

The 1972 ABM Treaty permitted the United States and Soviet Union to deploy ABM interceptors at two sites, one centered on the nation's capital and one containing ICBM silo launchers. Each site could contain up to 100 ground-based launchers for ABM interceptor missiles, along with specified radars and sensors. The ABM Treaty also obligated each nation not to develop, test, or deploy ABM systems for the "defense of the territory of its country" and not to provide a base for such a defense. It forbade testing and deployment of space-based, sea-based, or air-based ABM systems or components and it imposed a number of qualitative limits on missile defense programs. The Treaty, however, imposed no restrictions on defenses against aircraft, cruise missiles, or theater ballistic missiles.

In a Protocol signed in 1974, each side agreed that it would deploy an ABM system at only one site, either around the nation's capital or around an ICBM deployment area. The Soviet Union deployed its site around Moscow; this system has been maintained and upgraded over the years, and remains operational today. The United States deployed its ABM system around ICBM silo launchers located near Grand Forks, ND; it operated this facility briefly in 1974 before closing it down when it proved to be not cost effective.

The ABM Treaty was the source of considerable controversy and debate for most of its history. Presidents Reagan, George H. W. Bush, and Clinton all wrestled with the conflicting goals of defending the United States against ballistic missile attack while living within the confines of the ABM Treaty. President George W. Bush resolved this conflict in 2002, when he announced that the United States would withdraw from the ABM Treaty so that it could deploy ballistic missile defenses. The substance of this debate during the Clinton and Bush years is described in more detail below.

The Reagan and Bush Years: INF and START

During the election campaign of 1980, and after taking office in January 1981, President Ronald Reagan pledged to restore U.S. military capabilities, in general, and nuclear capabilities, in particular. He planned to expand U.S. nuclear forces and capabilities in an effort to counter the perceived Soviet advantages in nuclear weapons. Initially, at least, he rejected the use of arms control agreements to contain the Soviet threat. However, in 1982, after Congress and many analysts pressed for more diplomatic initiatives, the Reagan Administration outlined negotiating positions to address intermediate-range missiles, long-range strategic weapons, and ballistic missile defenses. These negotiations began to bear fruit in the latter half of President Reagan's second term, with the signing of the Intermediate-Range Nuclear Forces Treaty in 1987. President George H. W. Bush continued to pursue the first Strategic Arms Reduction Treaty (START), with the United States and Soviet Union signing this Treaty in July 1991. The collapse of the Soviet Union later that year led to calls for deeper reductions in strategic offensive arms. As a result, the United States and Russia signed START II in January 1993, weeks before the end of the Bush Administration.

The Intermediate-Range Nuclear Forces (INF) Treaty

In December 1979, NATO decided upon a "two track" approach to intermediate-range nuclear forces (INF) in Europe: it would seek negotiations with the Soviets to eliminate such systems, and at the same time schedule deployments as a spur to such negotiations. Negotiating sessions began in the fall of 1980 and continued until November 1983, when the Soviets left the talks upon deployment of the first U.S. INF systems in Europe. The negotiations resumed in January 1985. At the negotiations, the Reagan Administration called for a "double zero" option, which would eliminate all short- as well as long-range INF systems, a position at the time viewed by most observers to be unattractive to the Soviets. Nevertheless, significant progress occurred during the Gorbachev regime. At the Reykjavik summit in October 1986, Gorbachev agreed to include reductions of Soviet INF systems in Asia. In June 1987, the Soviets proposed a global ban on short- and long-range INF systems, which was similar to the U.S. proposal for a double zero. Gorbachev also accepted the U.S. proposal for an intrusive verification regime.

The United States and the Soviet Union signed the Treaty on Intermediate-Range Nuclear Forces (INF) on December 8, 1987. The INF Treaty was seen as a significant milestone in arms control because it established an intrusive verification regime and because it eliminated entire classes of weapons that both sides regarded as modern and effective. The United States and Soviet Union agreed to destroy all intermediate-range and shorter-range nuclear-armed ballistic missiles and ground-launched cruise missiles, which are those missiles with a range between 300 and 3,400 miles. The launchers associated with the controlled missiles were also to be destroyed. The signatories agreed that the warheads and guidance systems of the missiles need not be destroyed; they could be used or reconfigured for other systems not controlled by the Treaty.

The Soviets agreed to destroy approximately 1,750 missiles and the United States agreed to destroy 846 missiles, establishing a principle that asymmetrical reductions were acceptable in order to achieve a goal of greater stability. On the U.S. side, the principal systems destroyed were the Pershing II ballistic missile and the ground launched cruise missile (GLCM), both single-warhead systems. On the Soviet side, the principal system was the SS-20 ballistic missile, which carried three warheads. These systems, on both sides, were highly mobile and able to strike such high-value targets as command-and-control centers, staging areas, airfields, depots, and ports. The Soviets also agreed to destroy a range of older nuclear missiles, as well as the mobile, short-range SS-23, a system developed and deployed in the early 1980s. The parties had eliminated all their weapons by May 1991.

The verification regime of the INF Treaty permitted on-site inspections of selected missile assembly facilities and all storage centers, deployment zones, and repair, test, and elimination facilities. Although it did not permit "anywhere, anytime" inspections, it did allow up to 20 short-notice inspections of sites designated in the Treaty. The two sides agreed to an extensive data exchange, intended to account for all systems covered by the agreement. The Treaty also established a continuous portal monitoring procedure at one assembly facility in each country. Inspections under the INF Treaty continued until May 2001, however, the United States continues to operate its site at Russia's Votkinsk Missile Assembly facility under the terms of the 1991 START Treaty.

The INF Treaty returned to the news in 2007. Russia, partly in response to U.S. plans to deploy a missile defense radar in the Czech Republic and interceptor missiles in Poland, stated that it might withdraw from the INF Treaty. Some Russian officials have claimed this would allow Russia to deploy missiles with the range needed to threaten the missile defense system, in case it were capable of threatening Russia's strategic nuclear forces. Analysts outside Russia have also noted that Russia might be responding to concerns about the growing capabilities of China's missiles, or of those in other countries surrounding Russia.

In recent years, the United States has grown concerned about Russian activities that might be inconsistent with the INF Treaty. It has raised these issues with Russia, but has not received a satisfactory response. According to press reports, the United States has been monitoring the development of a new Russian ground-launched cruise missile since 2008, and concluded in late 2010 that it might be inconsistent with the treaty. The Administration plans to continue to address this issue with Russia, and has not yet made a formal declaration of Russian noncompliance with the treaty.

For Further Reading

CRS Issue Brief IB88003, *Arms Control: Ratification of the INF Treaty.* (Out of print. For copies contact Amy Woolf, 7-2379.)

CRS Issue Brief IB84131, *Verification and Compliance: Soviet Compliance with Arms Control Agreements.* (Out of print. For copies contact Amy Woolf, 7-2379.)

The Strategic Arms Reduction Treaty (START)

Like, INF, START negotiations began in 1982, but stopped between 1983 and 1985 after a Soviet walk-out in response to the U.S. deployment of intermediate range missiles in Europe. They resumed later in the Reagan Administration, and were concluded in the first Bush Administration. The United States and Soviet Union signed the first Strategic Arms Reduction Treaty (START) on July 31, 1991.

START After the Soviet Union

The demise of the Soviet Union in December 1991 immediately raised questions about the future of the Treaty. At that time, about 70% of the strategic nuclear weapons covered by START were deployed at bases in Russia; the other 30% were deployed in Ukraine, Kazakhstan, and Belarus.[4] Russia initially sought to be the sole successor to the Soviet Union for the Treaty, but the other three republics did not want to cede all responsibility for the Soviet Union's nuclear status and treaty obligations to Russia. In May 1992, the four republics and the United States signed a Protocol that made all four republics parties to the Treaty. At the same time, the leaders of Belarus, Ukraine, and Kazakhstan agreed to eliminate all of their nuclear weapons during the seven-year reduction period outlined in START. They also agreed to sign the Nuclear Non-Proliferation Treaty (NPT) as non-nuclear weapons states.

The U.S. Senate gave its consent to the ratification of START on October 1, 1992. The Russian parliament consented to the ratification of START on November 4, 1992, but it stated that Russia would not exchange the instruments of ratification for the Treaty until all three of the other republics adhered to the NPT as non-nuclear states. Kazakhstan completed the ratification process

---

[4] Leaders in these the non-Russian republics did not have control over the use of the nuclear weapons on their territory. Russian President Boris Yeltsin, and now Vladimir Putin, is the sole successor to the Soviet President in the command and control structure for Soviet nuclear weapons and he, along with his Minister of Defense and Military Chief of Staff, have the codes needed to launch Soviet nuclear weapons.

in June 1992 and joined the NPT as a non-nuclear weapon state on February 14, 1994. Belarus approved START and the NPT on February 4, 1993, and formally joined the NPT as a non-nuclear weapon state on July 22, 1993. Ukraine's parliament approved START in November 1993, but its approval was conditioned on Ukraine's retention of some of the weapons based on its territory and the provision of security guarantees by the other nuclear weapons states.

In early 1994, after the United States, Russia, and Ukraine agreed that Ukraine should receive compensation and security assurances in exchange for the weapons based on its soil, the parliament removed the conditions from its resolution of ratification. But it still did not approve Ukraine's accession to the NPT. The Ukrainian parliament took this final step on November 16, 1994, after insisting on and apparently receiving additional security assurances from the United States, Russia, and Great Britain. START officially entered into force with the exchange of the instruments of ratification on December 5, 1994.

START Provisions

START limits long-range nuclear forces—land-based intercontinental ballistic missiles (ICBMs), submarine-launched ballistic missiles (SLBMs), and heavy bombers—in the United States and the newly independent states of the former Soviet Union. Each side can deploy up to 6,000 *attributed* warheads on 1,600 ballistic missiles and bombers. (Some weapons carried on bombers do not count against the Treaty's limits, so each side could deploy 8,000 or 9,000 actual weapons.) Each side can deploy up to 4,900 warheads on ICBMs and SLBMs. Throughout the START negotiations, the United States placed a high priority on reductions in heavy ICBMs because they were thought to be able to threaten a first strike against U.S. ICBMs. Therefore, START also limits each side to 1,540 warheads on "heavy" ICBMs, a 50% reduction in the number of warheads deployed on the SS-18 ICBMs in the former Soviet republics.

START did not require the elimination of most of the missiles removed from service. The nations had to eliminate *launchers* for missiles that exceeded the permitted totals, but, in most cases, missiles could be placed in storage and warheads could either be stored or reused on missiles remaining in the force.

START contains a complex verification regime. Both sides collect most of the information needed to verify compliance with their own satellites and remote sensing equipment—the National Technical Means of Verification (NTM). But the parties also use data exchanges, notifications, and on-site inspections to gather information about forces and activities limited by the Treaty. Taken together, these measures are designed to provide each nation with the ability to deter and detect militarily significant violations. (No verification regime can ensure the detection of all violations. A determined cheater could probably find a way to conceal some types of violations.) Many also believe that the intrusiveness mandated by the START verification regime and the cooperation needed to implement many of these measures builds confidence and encourages openness among the signatories.

The United States and Russia completed the reductions in their forces by the designated date of December 5, 2001. All the warheads from 104 SS-18 ICBMs in Kazakhstan were removed and returned to Russia and all the launchers in that nation have been destroyed. Ukraine has destroyed all the SS-19 ICBM and SS-24 ICBM launchers on its territory and returned all the warheads from those missiles to Russia. Belarus had also returned to Russia all 81 SS-25 missiles and warheads based on its territory by late November 1996.

START Expiration

The START Treaty expired in December 2009. According to the terms of the Treaty, the parties could allow START to lapse, extend it without modification for another five years, or seek to modify the Treaty before extending it for five year intervals. The United States and Russia began, in 2006, to hold a series of discussions about the future of START, but, through the latter years of the Bush Administration, the two sides held sharply different views on what that future should be. Russian officials believed that the two nations should replace START with a new Treaty that would reduce the numbers of deployed warheads but contain many of the definitions, counting rules, and monitoring provisions of START. The Bush Administration rejected that approach; it noted that the new Moscow Treaty (described below) calls for further reductions in offensive nuclear weapons and it argued that many of the detailed provisions in START were no longer needed because the United States and Russia were no longer enemies. The United States suggested that the two sides reaffirm their commitment to the Moscow Treaty, and add to it an informal monitoring regime that would extend some of the monitoring and verification provisions in START. Analysts outside government have also suggested that the nations extend the monitoring provisions, at least through 2012, as the Moscow Treaty does not have its own verification regime. Some in the United States, however, object to this approach because some of the monitoring provisions have begun to impinge on U.S. strategic weapons and missile defense programs.

The Obama Administration altered the U.S. approach and has decided to negotiate a new Treaty that would replace START (this is discussed in more detail below). The United States and Russia began these discussions in April 2009, but were unable to complete them before START expired on December 5, 2009. As is noted, below, they did complete a New START Treaty in April 2010.

For Further Reading

CRS Report R40084, *Strategic Arms Control After START: Issues and Options*, by Amy F. Woolf.

CRS Report 91-492 F, *Cooperative Measures in START Verification*. (Out of print. For copies contact Amy Woolf, 7-2379.)

CRS Issue Brief IB98030, *Nuclear Arms Control: The U.S.-Russian Agenda*. (Out of print. For copies contact Amy Woolf, 7-2379.)

CRS Report 93-617 F, *START I and START II Arms Control Treaties: Background and Issues*. (Out of print. For copies contact Amy Woolf, 7-2379.)

START II

The United States and Russia signed the second START Treaty, START II, on January 3, 1993, after less than a year of negotiations. The Treaty never entered into force. Its consideration was delayed for several years during the 1990s, but it eventually received approval from both the U.S. Senate and Russian parliament. Nevertheless, it was overcome by events in 2002.

START II Provisions

START II would have limited each side to between 3,000 and 3,500 warheads; reductions initially were to occur by the year 2003 and would have been extended until 2007 if the nations had approved a new Protocol. It would have banned all MIRVed ICBMs and would have limited each side to 1,750 warheads on SLBMs.

To comply with these limits the United States would have removed two warheads (a process known as "downloading") from each of its 500 3-warhead Minuteman III missiles and eliminated all launchers for its 50 10-warhead MX missiles. The United States also stated that it would reduce its SLBM warheads by eliminating 4 Trident submarines and deploying the missiles on the 14 remaining Trident submarines with 5, rather than 8, warheads. Russia would have eliminated all launchers for its 10-warhead SS-24 missiles and 10-warhead SS-18 missiles. It would also have downloaded to a single warhead 105 6-warhead SS-19 missiles, if it retained those missiles. It would also have eliminated a significant number of ballistic missile submarines, both for budget reasons and to reduce to START II limits. These changes would have brought Russian forces below the 3,500 limit because so many of Russia's warheads are deployed on MIRVed ICBMs. As a result, many Russian officials and Duma members insisted that the United States and Russia negotiate a START III Treaty, with lower warhead numbers, so that Russia would not have to produce hundreds of new missiles to maintain START II levels.

START II implementation would have accomplished the long-standing U.S. objective of eliminating the Soviet SS-18 heavy ICBMs. The Soviet Union and Russia had resisted limits on these missiles in the past. Russia would have achieved its long-standing objective of limiting U.S. SLBM warheads, although the reductions would not have been as great as those for MIRVed ICBMs. The United States had long resisted limits on these missiles, but apparently believed a 50% reduction was a fair trade for the complete elimination of Russia's SS-18 heavy ICBMs.

START II would have relied on the verification regime established by START, with a few new provisions. For example, U.S. inspectors would be allowed to watch Russia pour concrete into the SS-18 silos and to measure the depth of the concrete when Russia converted the silos to hold smaller missiles. In addition, Russian inspectors could have viewed the weapons carriage areas on U.S. heavy bombers to confirm that the number of weapons the bombers are equipped to carry did not exceed the number attributed to that type of bomber.

START II Ratification

Although START II was signed in early January 1993, its full consideration was delayed until START entered into force at the end of 1994. The U.S. Senate further delayed its consideration during a Senate dispute over the future of the Arms Control and Disarmament Agency. The Senate eventually approved ratification of START II, by a vote of 87-4, on January 26, 1996.

The Russian Duma also delayed its consideration of START II. Many members of the Duma disapproved of the way the Treaty would affect Russian strategic offensive forces and many objected to the economic costs Russia would bear when implementing the treaty. The United States sought to address the Duma's concerns during 1997, by negotiating a Protocol that would extend the elimination deadlines in START II, and, therefore, reduce the annual costs of implementation, and by agreeing to negotiate a START III Treaty after START II entered into force. But this did not break the deadlock; the Duma again delayed its debate after the United States and Great Britain launched air strikes against Iraq in December 1998. The Treaty's future clouded again after the United States announced its plans in January 1999 to negotiate amendments to the 1972 ABM Treaty, and after NATO forces began their air campaign in Yugoslavia in April 1999.

President Putin offered his support to START II and pressed the Duma for action in early 2000. He succeeded in winning approval for the treaty on April 14 after promising, among other things, that Russia would withdraw from the Treaty if the United States withdrew from the 1972 ABM

Treaty. However, the Federal Law on Ratification said the Treaty could not enter into force until the United States approved ratification of several 1997 agreements related to the 1972 ABM Treaty. President Clinton never submitted these to the Senate, for fear they would be defeated. The Bush Administration also never submitted these to the Senate, announcing, instead, in June 2002, that the United States would withdraw from the ABM Treaty. Russia responded by announcing that it had withdrawn from START II and would not implement the Treaty's reductions.

For Further Reading

CRS Report 93-617 F, *START I and START II Arms Control Treaties: Background and Issues.* (Out of print. For copies contact Amy Woolf, 7-2379.)

CRS Report 97-359, *START II Debate in the Russian Duma: Issues and Prospects,* by Amy F. Woolf.

The Clinton and Bush Years: Moving Past START and the ABM Treaty

The arms control process between the United States and Russia essentially stalled during the 1990s, as efforts to ratify and implement START II dragged on. In 1997, in an effort to move the agenda forward, Presidents Clinton and Yeltsin agreed to a framework for a START III Treaty. But these negotiations never produced a Treaty, as the U.S.-Russian arms control agenda came to be dominated by U.S. plans for ballistic missile defenses and issues related to the ABM Treaty. When President Bush took office in 2001, he had little interest in pursuing formal arms control agreements with Russia. He signed the Strategic Offensive Reductions Treaty (known as the Moscow Treaty) in 2002, even though he would have preferred that the United States and Russia each set their force levels without any formal limits.

START III Framework for Strategic Offensive Forces

Many in Russia argued the United States and Russia should bypass START II and negotiate deeper reductions in nuclear warheads that were more consistent with the levels Russia was likely to retain in the future. The Clinton Administration did not want to set START II aside, in part because it wanted to be sure Russia eliminated its MIRVed ICBMS. However, many in the Administration eventually concluded that Russia would not ratify START II without some assurances that the warhead levels would decline further. So the United States agreed to proceed to START III, but *only after* START II entered into force; Presidents Clinton and Yeltsin agreed to this timeline in March 1997. The START III framework called for reductions to between 2,000 and 2,500 warheads for strategic offensive nuclear weapons on each side.

The United States and Russia held several rounds of discussions on START III, but they did not resolve their differences before the end of the Clinton Administration. President Bush did not pursue the negotiations after taking office in 2001. The demise of these discussions left many issues that had been central to the U.S.-Russian arms control process unresolved. For example, Presidents Clinton and Yeltsin had agreed to explore possible measures for limiting long-range, nuclear-armed, sea-launched cruise missiles and other tactical nuclear weapons in the START III framework. These weapons systems are not limited by existing treaties. Many in Congress have joined analysts outside the government in expressing concerns about the safety and security of Russia's stored nuclear weapons.

In addition, when establishing the START III framework, the United States and Russia agreed that they would explore proposals to enhance transparency and promote the irreversibility of warhead reductions. Many analysts viewed this step as critical to lasting, predictable reductions in nuclear weapons. The Bush Administration has, however, rejected this approach. Although it has pledged to eliminate some warheads removed from deployment, it will not offer any measures promoting the transparency or reversibility of this process. It wants to retain U.S. flexibility and the ability to restore warheads to deployed forces. Many critics of the Administration oppose this policy, in part, because it will undermine U.S. efforts to encourage Russia to eliminate warheads that might be at risk of loss or theft.

Ballistic Missile Defenses and the ABM Treaty

As was noted above, the 1972 Anti-Ballistic Missile (ABM) Treaty and 1974 Protocol allowed the United States and Soviet Union to deploy limited defenses against long-range ballistic missiles. The United States completed, then quickly abandoned a treaty-compliant ABM system near Grand Forks, ND, in 1974. The Soviet Union deployed, and Russia continues to operate, a treaty-compliant system around Moscow.

Missile Defense Plans and Programs

During the 1980s and early 1990s, the United States conducted research on a variety of ballistic missile defense technologies. In 1983 President Reagan collected and expanded these programs in the Strategic Defense Initiative (SDI), which sought to develop and deploy comprehensive missile defenses that would defend the United States against a deliberate, massive attack from the Soviet Union. The first Bush Administration changed this focus, seeking instead to provide a defense against possible limited missile attacks that might arise from any number of countries throughout the world.

After the Persian Gulf War in 1991, with Iraq's attacks with Scud missiles alerting many to the dangers of missile proliferation and the threats posed by short- and medium-range theater ballistic missiles, the United States began developing several advanced theater missile defense (TMD) systems. At the same time, the Clinton Administration pursued research and technology development for national missile defenses (NMD). The Department of Defense concluded that there was no military requirement for the deployment of such a system after intelligence estimates found that no additional nations (beyond China, Russia, France, and Great Britain) were likely to develop missiles that could threaten the continental United States for at least the next 10-15 years. However, after a congressionally mandated commission raised concerns about the proliferation of long-range missiles in July 1998 and North Korea tested a three-stage missile in August 1998, the Clinton Administration began to consider the deployment of an NMD, with a program structured to achieve that objective in 2005. On September 1, 2000, after disappointing test results, President Clinton announced that he would not authorize construction needed to begin deployment of an NMD.

President George W. Bush altered U.S. policy on missile defenses. His Administration has sought to develop a layered defense, with land-based, sea-based, and space-based components, that could protect the United States, its allies, and its forces overseas from short, medium, and long-range ballistic missiles. It has begun to deploy land-based missile interceptors for defense against long-range missiles in Alaska and California, and has pursued the deployment of defenses against shorter-range missiles on naval ships. The Administration declared the interceptors in Alaska to be operational in late 2004, but their status and capabilities remain uncertain.

ABM Treaty Issues and Negotiations

The missile defense systems advocated by the Reagan and first Bush Administrations would not have been permitted under the ABM Treaty. In 1985, the United States proposed, in negotiations with the Soviet Union, that the two sides replace the ABM Treaty with an agreement that would permit deployment of more extensive defenses. These negotiations failed, and, in 1993, the Clinton Administration altered their focus. It sought a demarcation agreement to clarify the difference between theater missile defenses and strategic missile defenses so the United States could proceed with theater missile defense (TMD) programs without raising questions about compliance with the Treaty.

The United States and Russia signed two joint statements on ABM/TMD Demarcation in September 1997. As amendments to the ABM Treaty, these agreements required the advice and consent of the Senate before they entered into force. But President Clinton never submitted them to the Senate, knowing that the required 67 votes would prove elusive as many of the Senators in the Republican majority believed the ABM Treaty, even if modified, would stand in the way of the deployment of robust missile defenses.

In February 1999, the United States and Russia began to discuss ABM Treaty modifications that would permit deployment of a U.S. national missile defense (NMD) system. The United States sought to reassure Russia that the planned NMD would not interfere with Russia's strategic nuclear forces and that the United States still viewed the ABM Treaty as central to the U.S.-Russian strategic balance. The Russians were reportedly unconvinced, noting that the United States could expand its system so that it could intercept a significant portion of Russia's forces. They also argued that the United States had overstated the threat from rogue nations. Furthermore, after Russia approved START II, President Putin noted that U.S. withdrawal from the ABM Treaty would lead not only to Russian withdrawal from START II, but also Russian withdrawal from a wider range of arms control agreements. Through the end of the Clinton Administration, Russia refused to consider U.S. proposals for modifications to the ABM Treaty. Some argued that Russia's position reflected its belief that the United States would not withdraw from the ABM Treaty and, therefore, if Russia refused to amend it, the United States would not deploy national missile defenses.

Officials in the new Bush Administration referred to the ABM Treaty as a relic of the Cold War and the President stated that the United States would need to move beyond the limits in the Treaty to deploy robust missile defenses. In discussions that began in the middle of 2001, the Bush Administration sought to convince Russia to accept a U.S. proposal for the nations to "set aside" the Treaty together. The Administration also offered Russia extensive briefings to demonstrate that its missile defense program would not threaten Russia but that the ABM Treaty would interfere with the program. Russia would not agree to set the Treaty aside, and, instead, suggested that the United States identify modifications to the Treaty that would allow it to pursue the more robust testing program contained in its proposals. But, according to some reports, Russia would have insisted on the right to determine whether proposed tests were consistent with the Treaty. The Bush Administration would not accept these conditions and President Bush announced, on December 13, 2001, that the United States would withdraw from the ABM Treaty. This withdrawal took effect on June 13, 2002. Russia's President Putin stated that this action was "mistaken." Russia responded by withdrawing from the START II Treaty, but this action was largely symbolic as the Treaty seemed likely to never enter into force.

In addition to deploying long-range missile defense interceptors in Alaska and California, the Bush Administration proposed that the United States deploy a third missile defense site in Europe to defend against a potential Iranian missile threat. The system was to include 10 interceptors based in Poland and a radar in the Czech Republic. Russia's former President Putin and his successor, Vladimir Medvedev, argued that the proposal would reignite the arms race and upset U.S.-Russian-European security relations. U.S. officials disputed Russia's objections, noting that the interceptors would not be able to intercept Russian missiles or undermine Russia's deterrent capabilities. In mid-2007, Russia offered to cooperate on missile defense, proposing the use of a Russian-leased radar in Azerbaijan, but urging that U.S. facilities not be built in Eastern Europe. President Bush welcomed the idea in principle, but insisted upon the need for the European sites. Despite ongoing discussions over the issue, sharp Russian criticism of the program continued. Medvedev said that Russia might deploy Iskander tactical missiles to Kaliningrad, but later stated that Moscow would not do so if the United States reversed its plan to emplace GMD facilities in Poland and the Czech Republic.

Congress resisted the Bush Administration's request for funding for this system. It withheld much of the funding, pending at least two successful tests and the completion of agreements with the Polish and Czech governments. It also requested further reports on the need for and capabilities of the proposed system.

The Obama Administration reviewed and restructured U.S. plans for a missile defense site in Europe. On September 17, 2009, the Administration announced it would cancel the system proposed by the Bush Administration. Instead, Defense Secretary Gates announced U.S. plans to develop and deploy a regional BMD capability that could be deployed around the world on relatively short notice during crises or as the situation may demand. Gates argued this new capability, based primarily around current BMD sensors and interceptors, would be more responsive and adaptable to growing concern over the direction of Iranian short- and medium-range ballistic missile proliferation. This capability would continue to evolve and expand over the next decade, as the United States moved forward with the concept known as the "Phased Adaptive Approach." As missile threats matured during the next decade, the missile defense system would include interceptors that could respond against more numerous and more sophisticated threats.

For Further Reading

CRS Report RL34051, *Long-Range Ballistic Missile Defense in Europe*, by Steven A. Hildreth and Carl Ek.

CRS Report RL31111, *Missile Defense: The Current Debate*, by Steven A. Hildreth et al.

CRS Report 98-496, *Anti-Ballistic Missile Treaty Demarcation and Succession Agreements: Background and Issues*, by Amy F. Woolf.

CRS Issue Brief IB98030, *Nuclear Arms Control: The U.S. Russian Agenda*. (Out of print. For copies contact Amy Woolf, 7-2379.)

The Strategic Offensive Reductions Treaty

During a summit meeting with President Putin in November 2001, President Bush announced that the United States would reduce its "operationally deployed" strategic nuclear warheads to a level between 1,700 and 2,200 warheads during the next decade. He stated that the United States would reduce its forces unilaterally, without signing a formal agreement. President Putin indicated that Russia wanted to use the formal arms control process, emphasizing that the two sides should focus on "reaching a reliable and verifiable agreement." Russia sought a "legally binding document" that would provide "predictability and transparency" and ensure for the "irreversibilty of the reduction of nuclear forces." The United States wanted to maintain the flexibility to size and structure its nuclear forces in response to its own needs. It preferred a less formal process, such as an exchange of letters and, possibly, new transparency measures that would allow each side to understand the force structure plans of the other side.

Within the Bush Administration, Secretary of State Powell supported the conclusion of a "legally binding" agreement because he believed it would help President Putin's standing with his domestic critics. He apparently prevailed over the objections of officials in the Pentagon. Although the eventual outcome did differ from the initial approach of the Bush Administration, most observers agree that it did not undermine the fundamental U.S. objectives in the negotiations because the Treaty's provisions would not impede the Bush Administration's plans for U.S. strategic nuclear forces.

The United States and Russia signed the Strategic Offensive Reductions Treaty on May 24, 2002. The U.S. Senate gave its advice and consent to the ratification of the Treaty on March 6, 2003. The Russian Duma approved the Federal Law on Ratification for the Treaty on May 14, 2003. The Treaty entered into force on June 1, 2003. The Treaty was due to remain in force until December 31, 2012, after which it could be extended or replaced by another agreement. It lapsed, however, on February 5, 2011, when the New START Treaty (see below) entered into force.

Treaty Provisions

Article I contains the only limit in the Treaty, stating that the United States and Russia will reduce their "strategic nuclear warheads" to between 1,700 and 2,200 warheads by December 31, 2012. The text does not define "strategic nuclear warheads" and, therefore, does not indicate whether the parties will count only those warheads that are "operationally deployed," all warheads that would count under the START counting rules, or some other quantity of nuclear warheads. The text does refer to statements made by Presidents Bush and Putin in November and December 2001, when each outlined their own reduction plans. This reference may indicate that the United States and Russia could each use their own definition when counting strategic nuclear warheads. The Treaty does not limit delivery vehicles or impose sublimits on specific types of weapons systems. Each party shall determine its own "composition and structure of its strategic offensive arms."

Monitoring and Verification

The Strategic Offensive Reductions Treaty does not contain any monitoring or verification provisions. The Bush Administration noted that the United States and Russia already collected information about strategic nuclear forces under START I and during implementation of the Nunn-Lugar Cooperative Threat Reduction Program. Some in Congress questioned, however, whether this information would be sufficient for the duration of the Treaty, since START I was due to expire in 2009, three years before the end of implementation under the new Treaty.

Nonstrategic Nuclear Weapons

The Strategic Offensive Reductions Treaty also does not contain any limits or restrictions on nonstrategic nuclear weapons. Yet, as was noted above, many Members of Congress have argued that these weapons pose a greater threat to the United States and its allies than strategic nuclear weapons. During hearings before the Senate Foreign Relations Committee, Secretary of Defense Rumsfeld and Secretary of State Powell both agreed that the disposition of nonstrategic nuclear weapons should be on the agenda for future meetings between the United States and Russia, although neither supported a formal arms control regime to limit or contain these weapons. These discussions have not occurred, and many analysts outside government have renewed their calls for reductions in nonstrategic nuclear weapons.

For Further Reading

CRS Report RL31448, *Nuclear Arms Control: The Strategic Offensive Reductions Treaty*, by Amy F. Woolf

CRS Report RL31222, *Arms Control and Strategic Nuclear Weapons: Unilateral vs. Bilateral Reductions*, by Amy F. Woolf

---

The Obama Administration: New START

The United States and Russia began to discuss their options for arms control after START in mid-2006. During the Bush Administration, they were unable to agree on a path forward. Neither side wanted to extend START in its original form, as some of the Treaty's provisions had begun to interfere with some military programs on both sides. Russia wanted to replace START with a new Treaty that would further reduce deployed forces while using many of the same definitions and counting rules in START. The United States initially did not want to negotiate a new treaty, but, under the Bush Administration, would have been willing to extend, informally, some of START's monitoring provisions. In 2008, the Bush Administration agreed to conclude a new Treaty, with monitoring provisions attached, but this Treaty would have resembled the far less formal Strategic Offensive Reductions Treaty. In December 2008, the two sides agreed that they wanted to replace START before it expired, but acknowledged that this task would have to be left to negotiations between Russia and the Obama Administration.

Pursuing an Agreement

The United States and Russia began to hold talks on a new treaty during the first few months of the Obama Administration. In early March 2009, Secretary of State Hillary Clinton and Russia's Foreign Minister Sergey Lavrov agreed that the two nations would seek to reach an agreement that would replace START by the end of 2009. In April, after their meeting in London prior to the G-20 summit, Presidents Obama and Medvedev endorsed these negotiations and their goal of reaching an agreement by the end of 2009. When Presidents Obama and Medvedev met in Moscow on July 6-7, 2009, they signed a Joint Understanding for the START follow-on Treaty. This statement contained a range for the numerical limits that would be in the Treaty—between 500 and 1,100 of strategic delivery vehicles and between 1,500 and 1,675 for their associated warheads. It also included a list of other issues—such as provisions for calculating the limits, provisions on definitions, and a provision on the relationship between strategic offensive and strategic defensive weapons—that will be addressed in the Treaty.

START expired on December 5, 2009. At the time, the negotiating teams continued to meet in Geneva, but the negotiations concluded shortly before the end of 2009 without reaching a final agreement. The formal talks resumed in late January 2010, and the parties concluded the New START Treaty on early April 2010. Presidents Obama and Medvedev signed the Treaty in Prague on April 8, 2010; it entered into force on February 5, 2011.

Treaty Provisions

Limits on Warheads and Launchers

The New START Treaty contains three central limits on U.S. and Russian strategic offensive nuclear forces. First, it limits each side to no more than 800 deployed and nondeployed ICBM and SLBM launchers and deployed and nondeployed heavy bombers equipped to carry nuclear armaments. Second, within that total, it limits each side to no more than 700 deployed ICBMs, deployed SLBMs, and deployed heavy bombers equipped to carry nuclear armaments. Third, the treaty limits each side to no more than 1,550 deployed warheads. Deployed warheads include the actual number of warheads carried by deployed ICBMs and SLBMs, and one warhead for each deployed heavy bomber equipped for nuclear armaments.

According to New START's Protocol, a deployed ICBM launcher is "an ICBM launcher that contains an ICBM and is not an ICBM test launcher, an ICBM training launcher, or an ICBM launcher located at a space launch facility." A deployed SLBM launcher is a launcher installed on an operational submarine that contains an SLBM and is not intended for testing or training. A deployed mobile launcher of ICBMs is one that contains an ICBM and is not a mobile test launcher or a mobile launcher of ICBMs located at a space launch facility. These deployed launchers can be based only at ICBM bases. A deployed ICBM or SLBM is one that is contained in a deployed launcher. A deployed heavy bomber is one that is equipped for nuclear armaments but is not a "test heavy bomber or a heavy bomber located at a repair facility or at a production facility." Moreover, a heavy bomber is equipped for nuclear armaments if it is "equipped for long-range nuclear ALCMs, nuclear air-to-surface missiles, or nuclear bombs." Nondeployed launchers are, therefore, those that are used for testing or training, those that are located at space launch facilities, or those that are located at deployment areas or on submarines but do not contain a deployed ICBM or SLBM.

The warhead limits in New START differ from those in the original START Treaty. First, the original START Treaty contained several sublimits on warheads attributed to different types of strategic weapons, in part because the United States wanted the treaty to impose specific limits on elements of the Soviet force that were deemed to be "destabilizing." New START, in contrast, contains only a single limit on the aggregate number of deployed warheads. This provides each nation with the freedom to mix their forces as they see fit. This change reflects, in part, a lesser concern with Cold War models of strategic and crisis stability. It also derives from the U.S. desire to maintain flexibility in determining the structure of its own nuclear forces.

Second, under START, to calculate the number of warheads that counted against the treaty limits, the United States and Russia counted deployed launchers, assumed launcher contained an operational missile, and assumed each missile carried an "attributed" number of warheads. The number of warheads attributed to each missile or bomber was the same for all missiles and bombers of that type. The parties then multiplied these warhead numbers by the number of deployed ballistic missiles and heavy bombers to determine the number of warheads that counted under the treaty's limits. Under New START, the United States and Russia will also count the number of deployed launchers. But they will not calculate the number of deployed warheads by multiplying the number of launchers by a warhead attribution number. Instead, each side will simply declare the total number of warheads deployed across their force. This counting method will provide the United States with the flexibility to reduce its forces without eliminating launchers and to structure its deployed forces to meet evolving operational needs.

Monitoring and Verification

The New START Treaty contains a monitoring and verification regime that resembles the regime in START, in that its text contains detailed definitions of items limited by the treaty; provisions governing the use of NTM to gather data on each side's forces and activities; an extensive database that identifies the numbers, types, and locations of items limited by the treaty; provisions requiring notifications about items limited by the treaty; and inspections allowing the parties to confirm information shared during data exchanges. At the same time, the verification regime has been streamlined to make it less costly and complex than the regime in START. It also has been adjusted to reflect the limits in New START and the current circumstances in the relationship between the United States in Russia. In particular, it focuses on maintaining transparency, cooperation, and openness, as well as on deterring and detecting potential violations.

Under New START, the United States and Russia continue to rely on their NTM to collect information about the numbers and locations of their strategic forces. They may also broadcast and exchange telemetry—the data generated during missile flight tests—up to five times each year. They do not need this data to monitor compliance with any particular limits in New START, but the telemetry exchange will provide some transparency into the capabilities of their systems.[5] The parties will also exchange a vast amount of data about those forces, specifying not only their distinguishing characteristics, but also their precise locations and the number of warheads deployed on each deployed delivery vehicle. They will notify each other, and update the database, whenever they move forces between declared facilities. The treaty also requires the parties to display their forces, and allows each side to participate in exhibitions, to confirm information listed in the database.

Under New START, each party can conduct up to 18 short-notice, on-site inspections each year; both sides used this full quote of inspections during the three years of the treaty's implementation. The treaty divides these into Type One inspections and Type Two inspections. Each side can conduct up to 10 Type One inspections and up to eight Type Two inspections. Moreover, during each Type One inspection, the parties will be able to perform two different types of inspection activities—these are essentially equivalent to the data update inspections and reentry vehicle inspections in the original START Treaty. As a result, the 18 short-notice inspections permitted under New START are essentially equivalent to the 28 short-notice inspections permitted under START.

Relationship Between Offensive and Defensive Weapons

In the Joint Understanding signed at the Moscow summit in July 2009, the United States and Russia agreed that the new treaty would contain a "provision on the interrelationship of strategic offensive arms and strategic defensive arms." This statement, which appears in the preamble to

---

[5] U.S. State Department, Bureau of Verification, Compliance and Implementation, *Telemetry*, Fact Sheet, Washington, DC, April 8, 2010, http://www.state.gov/t/vci/rls/139904 htm.

New START, states that the parties recognize "the existence of the interrelationship between strategic offensive arms and strategic defensive arms, that this interrelationship will become more important as strategic nuclear arms are reduced, and that current strategic defensive arms do not undermine the viability and effectiveness of the strategic offensive arms of the parties." Russia and the United States each issued unilateral statements when they signed New START that clarified their positions on the relationship between New START and missile defenses. Russia indicated that it might exercise its right to withdraw from the treaty if the United States increased the capabilities of its missile defenses "in such a way that threatens the potential of the strategic nuclear forces of the Russian Federation." The United States responded by noting that its "missile defense systems are not intended to affect the strategic balance with Russia. The United States missile defense systems would be employed to defend the United States against limited missile launches, and to defend its deployed forces, allies and partners against regional threats."

Officials from the Obama Administration testified to the Senate and repeatedly emphasized that these statements did not impose any obligations on either the United States or Russia and would not result in any limits on U.S. missile defense programs. These statements also did not provide Russia with "veto power" over U.S. missile defense systems. Although Russia has said it may withdraw from the treaty if the U.S. missile defenses threaten "the potential of the strategic nuclear forces of the Russian Federation," the United States has no obligation to consult with Russia to confirm that its planned defenses do not cross this threshold. It may develop and deploy whatever defenses it chooses; Russia can then determine, for itself, whether those defenses affect its strategic nuclear forces and whether it thinks the threat to those forces justifies withdrawal from the treaty.

For Further Reading

CRS Report R41219, *The New START Treaty: Central Limits and Key Provisions*, by Amy F. Woolf

CRS Report R41201, *Monitoring and Verification in Arms Control*, by Amy F. Woolf

CRS Report R43037, *Next Steps in Nuclear Arms Control with Russia: Issues for Congress*, by Amy F. Woolf

---

Threat Reduction and Nonproliferation Assistance

As the Soviet Union collapsed in late 1991, many Members of Congress grew concerned that deteriorating social and economic conditions in Russia would affect control over Soviet weapons of mass destruction. In December 1991, Congress authorized the transfer of $400 million from the FY1992 Department of Defense (DOD) budget to help the republics that inherited the Soviet nuclear and chemical weapons stockpile—Russia, Kazakhstan, Ukraine, and Belarus—transport and dismantle these weapons. This effort has since grown substantially, with Congress appropriating more than $1 billion each year, in recent years for nonproliferation and threat reduction programs administered by the Department of Defense (DOD), the State Department, and the Department of Energy (DOE). The United States has also worked with other nations, through the G-8 Global Partnership, to expand participation in, and funding for, nonproliferation and threat reduction programs in Russia.

DOD's Cooperative Threat Reduction Program (CTR)

At its inception, DOD's CTR program sought to provide Russia, Ukraine, Belarus, and Kazakhstan with assistance in the safe and secure transportation, storage, and dismantlement of nuclear weapons. During the first few years, the mandate for U.S. assistance expanded to include efforts to secure materials that might be used in nuclear or chemical weapons, to prevent the diversion of scientific expertise from the former Soviet Union, to expand military-to-military contacts between officers in the United States and the former Soviet Union, and to facilitate the demilitarization of defense industries. In the late 1990s, Congress added funds to the CTR budget for biological weapons proliferation prevention; this effort has expanded substantially in recent years. Congress also expanded the CTR program to allow the use of CTR funds for emergency assistance to remove weapons of mass destruction or materials and equipment related to these weapons from any of the former Soviet republics.

CTR Implementation

Initial implementation of the Cooperative Threat Reduction (CTR) Program was slowed by administrative requirements on the U.S. side; the complex nature of activities being undertaken; the need for major changes in the attitudes of recipients toward the United States and the idea of weapons dismantlement and destruction; and political and economic upheavals within and among the states of the former Soviet Union. For example, before funds could be obligated for specific projects, the United States had to sign general "umbrella" agreements with each recipient nation that set out the privileges and immunities of U.S. personnel and the legal and customs framework for the provision of the aid.

The umbrella agreement between the United States and Russia was renewed twice, but lapsed in June 2013. Although it was replaced with a bilateral protocol under the Multilateral Nuclear Environmental Program in the Russian Federation Agreement (MNEPR), the scope of cooperation between the two sides has narrowed considerably.

The United States has provided Russia and the other former Soviet states with assistance on several different types of projects. For example, the United States has provided extensive assistance with projects designed to help with the elimination of nuclear, chemical, and other weapons and their delivery vehicles. These projects have helped Russia, Ukraine, Belarus, and Kazakhstan remove warheads, deactivate missiles, and eliminate launch facilities for nuclear weapons covered by the START Treaty. Several projects were designed to enhance the safety, security and control over nuclear weapons and fissile materials. These projects provided Russia with bullet-proof Kevlar blankets, secure canisters, and improved rail cars for warheads transported from Ukraine, Belarus, and Kazakhstan to storage and dismantlement facilities in Russia. The CTR program also funded several projects at storage facilities for nuclear weapons and materials, to improve security and accounting systems and to provide storage space for plutonium removed from nuclear warheads when they are dismantled. Some projects also encouraged Russia, Kazakhstan, and Ukraine to convert military efforts to peaceful purposes. Many of these projects were nearing completion, and the United States will no longer fund them after 2013.

Chemical Weapons Destruction

The United States and Russia used CTR funds to construct a chemical weapons destruction facility at Shchuch'ye. This facility is intended to help Russia comply with its obligations under the Chemical Weapons convention and to prevent the loss or theft of Soviet-era chemical weapons by ensuring their safe and secure destruction. Construction on this facility began in March 2003. The United States also helped install equipment at the destruction facility and to train the operating personnel. The United States and Russia had hoped that construction would be completed and the facility would begin operations by the end of 2008. It would then take around 3½ years to destroy the stocks of nerve agent, allowing Russia to meet the 2012 deadline. Operations at the facility began in March 2009, and it was officially dedicated in late May 2009. At the end of 2012, Russia had used it to eliminate over 3,321.5 metric tons of nerve agent.

Cooperative Biological Engagement

The Soviet Union reportedly developed the world's largest biological weapons program, employing an estimated 60,000 people at more than 50 sites. Russia reportedly continued to pursue research and development of biological agents in the 1990s, even as the security systems and supporting infrastructure at its facilities began to deteriorate. The United State began to provide Russia with CTR assistance to improve safety and security at its biological weapons sites and to help employ biological weapons scientists during the late 1990s. Much of the work in Russia and other states of the former Soviet Union focused on safe and secure storage and handling of biological pathogen collections. These programs are likely to lapse with the expiration of the memorandum of understanding in June 2013. In recent years, the United States has expanded its biological engagement programs beyond the former Soviet Union, and now works globally to secure pathogen collections, train scientists on security issues, and improve disease surveillance. The Obama Administration has stated that the goal of the CBE program is to counter the "threat of state and non-state actors acquiring biological materials and expertise that could be used to develop or deploy a biological weapon." In the FY2014 budget request, biological weapons engagement programs accounted for nearly 60% of the CTR budget.

Scope and Priorities for CTR Projects

The initial Nunn-Lugar legislation was tightly focused on the transport, storage, and destruction of weapons of mass destruction. But the focus of CTR funding has changed, as the program evolves. Much of the work on strategic offensive arms reductions has been completed, and a growing proportion of the funding is focused on securing and eliminating chemical and biological weapons. Over the past decade, the United States has also viewed the CTR program, and other U.S. nonproliferation assistance to the former Soviet states, as a part of its efforts to keep weapons of mass destruction away from terrorists. This objective altered some of the funding priorities, with a growing number of projects focused on border and export control.

As much of the work has been completed on securing and eliminating Soviet legacy nuclear weapons and constructing the chemical weapons destruction facility, funding has shifted into projects that seek to prevent the proliferation of biological weapons. Moreover, a small but increasing proportion of CTR funding is now allocated to projects outside the former Soviet Union, as the United States seeks to engage a greater number of nations as partners in the effort to secure vulnerable nuclear materials and other weapons of mass destruction.

Future of the CTR Program

The United States and Russia initially signed the Memorandum of Understanding, known as the Umbrella Agreement, that governs implementation of CTR projects in 1992. This agreement had an initial seven-year duration and was renewed in 1999 and 2006. It expired in June 2013. The United States and Russia have replaced it with a bilateral protocol under the Multilateral Nuclear Environmental Program in the Russian Federation Agreement (MNEPR). Russia's Ministry of Defense will no longer participate in these cooperative programs. As a result, many of the CTR projects in Russia will wind down, although the two countries will continue to cooperate on some areas of nuclear security. The United States will also continue to fund cooperative engagement programs in countries around the world.

For Further Reading

CRS Report R43143, *The Evolution of Cooperative Threat Reduction: Issues for Congress*, by Mary Beth D. Nikitin and Amy F. Woolf

---

Department of Energy Nonproliferation Cooperation Programs

The Department of Energy has contributed to U.S. threat reduction and nonproliferation assistance to the former Soviet states from the start, when CTR included a small amount of funding for materials control and protection. Since then, the United States and Russia have been cooperating, through several programs, to secure and eliminate many of the materials that could help terrorists or rogue nations acquire their own nuclear capabilities.

Highly Enriched Uranium

Highly enriched uranium from dismantled weapons is relatively easy to dispose of, since it can be diluted to low-enriched uranium which is directly usable in current operating power reactors. In February 1993 the United States and Russia agreed that highly enriched uranium from weapons would be diluted to a low enrichment level suitable for use in commercial nuclear power reactors. The United States has agreed to purchase 500 metric tons of HEU from Russia's dismantled nuclear warheads, and deliveries have started to the U.S. Enrichment Corporation, which supplies uranium fuel for domestic and foreign reactors. By September 2005 about 250 metric tons of HEU had been recycled, at a purchase price of about $4 billion, according to USEC. The 500-ton total is expected to be completed by 2013.

Plutonium Disposition

In the Plutonium Management and Disposition Agreement, signed in September 2000, each side agreed to dispose of 34 metric tons of weapons-grade plutonium, and to do so at roughly the same time. The parties could use two methods for disposing of the plutonium—they could either convert it to mixed oxide fuel (MOX) for nuclear power reactors or immobilize it and dispose of it in a way that would preclude its use in nuclear weapons. Russia has expressed little interest in the permanent disposal of plutonium, noting that the material could have great value for its civilian power program. The United States initially intended to pursue both options. However, after reviewing U.S. nonproliferation policies in 2001, the Bush Administration concluded that this approach would be too costly. Instead, it outlined a plan for the United States to convert almost all its surplus plutonium to MOX fuel.

In late July 2003, the Bush Administration announced that the plutonium disposition program would not pursue additional contracts in 2004 because the United States and Russia were unable to agree on the liability provisions for a new implementing agreement for the program. The two nations reportedly reached an a liability agreement in 2005, although it has not yet been signed by Russia's President Putin. Russia has indicated that it may not pursue the MOX program to eliminate its plutonium, opting, instead for the construction of fast breeder reactors that could burn plutonium directly for energy production. The United States is not likely to fund this effort, as many in the United States argue that breeder reactors, which produce more plutonium than

---

they consume, would undermine nonproliferation objectives. Moreover, the cost of the U.S. MOX facility has escalated in recent years, and DOE has considered cancelling the program.

Materials Protection, Control, and Accounting

Many in the United States have expressed concerns about the safety and security of nuclear materials located at civilian research facilities in the former Soviet Union. Government-to-government projects at facilities that housed nuclear materials began in 1994. In a parallel effort that sought to reduce delays in these projects, experts from the U.S. nuclear laboratories, which are a part of DOE, also began less formal contacts with their counterparts in Russia to identify and solve safety and security problems at Russian facilities. Together, these government-to-government and lab-to-lab projects evolved into an effort to apply Material Protection, Control and Accounting (MPC&A) techniques to Russian facilities.

According to the Department of Energy, the MPC&A program has provided assistance at more than 50 facilities in the former Soviet Union. At many of these facilities, the program focused on providing upgrades to security to reduce the risk of a loss of materials. These upgrades include the installation of improved security systems that use modern technology and strict material control and accounting systems. The program has also provided security training for Russian nuclear specialists. During the past decade, the United States expanded the program to include efforts to secure radiological materials that would not be suitable for nuclear weapons but could be used in radiological dispersal devices, and to improve border security and monitoring to discourage and detect illicit efforts to transfer these materials.

Access to Russian Facilities

A GAO study released in early 2003 noted that Russia continues to deny the United States access to many facilities that are a part of the weapons complex maintained by Russia's Ministry of Atomic Affairs (MINATOM). As a result, the United States cannot even begin to address security and accounting concerns for a majority of the nuclear materials at risk in Russia. In addition, because access problems have slowed program implementation, DOE maintains significant balances of unallocated funds from prior years. Congress has expressed concerns about these funds, particularly as it adds more money to DOE's budget for nonproliferation programs.

For Further Reading

CRS Report R43143, *The Evolution of Cooperative Threat Reduction: Issues for Congress*, by Mary Beth D. Nikitin and Amy F. Woolf

---

State Department Programs

After the collapse of the Soviet Union in 1991, many experts feared that scientists from Russia's nuclear weapons complex might sell their knowledge to other nations seeking nuclear weapons. Many of these scientists had worked in the Soviet Union's "closed" nuclear cities where they had enjoyed relatively high salaries and prestige, but their jobs evaporated during Russia's economic and political crises in the early 1990s. Even those scientists who retained their jobs saw their incomes decline sharply as Russia was unable to pay their salaries for months at a time. In response to these concerns, the United States, Japan, the European Union, and Russia established the International Science and Technology Center (ISTC) in Moscow. A similar center began operating in Kiev in 1993. In subsequent years, several other former Soviet states have joined and other nations have added their financial support.

The science center programs also began as a part of DOD's CTR program, and were moved to the State Department budget in 1996. The centers fund scientists who have worked on nuclear, chemical, and biological weapons, but they have, historically, focused on nuclear scientists, with many projects going to those who work at institutes in the closed nuclear cities. The State Department estimates that about half of the participants are senior scientists, which means the programs may have reached a significant portion of the estimated 30,000 to 70,000 senior scientists and engineers in the Soviet nuclear complex. However, most of these scientists spend fewer than 50 days per year on projects funded by the science centers. In the remainder of the time, most continue to work at their primary jobs.

The Russian government announced in August 2010 that it would withdraw from the agreement on the establishing of the ISTC, and from the protocol on temporary application of the ISTC foundation agreement. The ISTC Board decided in December 2010 that all current projects with Russia would be completed, and that Russia would not withdraw before 2014. All other member states reaffirmed their commitment to their countries' participation. The ISTC Board approved Kazakhstan's offer to host the ISTC main office in December 2012, and a transition is underway.

The collapse of political control along the Soviet borders, along with incentives created by the weakness in the economies of the newly independent states, contribute to concerns about the potential for smuggling or illegal exports of materials and technology from the former Soviet Union. The State Department's Export Control and Related Border Security Assistance (EXBS) program helps the former Soviet states and other nations improve their ability to interdict nuclear smuggling and their ability to stop the illicit trafficking of all materials for weapons of mass destruction, along with dual use goods and technologies. The EXBS program currently has projects underway in more than 30 nations, and is expanding its reach around the globe.

For Further Reading

CRS Report R43143, *The Evolution of Cooperative Threat Reduction: Issues for Congress*, by Mary Beth D. Nikitin and Amy F. Woolf

---

G-8 Global Partnership Against the Spread of Weapons and Materials of Mass Destruction

Since the creation of the Nunn-Lugar program in 1992, the United States has pressed its allies to provide similar support to Russia and the other former Soviet states. Like the United States, the G-8 countries faced difficulties in implementing similar programs. In early 2002, the United States proposed to the G-8 an expansion of its Cooperative Threat Reduction programs called "10 plus 10 over 10"—that is, the other G-8 countries (including Russia) would add $10 billion more over 10 years to the $10 billion the United States was already planning to spend on CTR-related programs. By expanding the programs to include more donors, the participants would not only be able to increase their level of effort in Russia, but might also be able to address potential proliferation problems in other nations.

At their June 2002 summit at Kananaskis, the Group of Eight (United States, Canada, UK, France, Germany, Italy, Japan (G-7) plus Russia (G-8)) formed the Global Partnership (GP) Against the Spread of Weapons and Materials of Mass Destruction. Under this partnership, the

United States, other members of the G-7 and the European Union have agreed to raise up to $20 billion over 10 years for projects beginning in Russia related to disarmament, nonproliferation, counterterrorism, and nuclear safety. The Global Partnership has spurred Russia to take on a greater portion of the financial burden for these projects, as second-largest donor. According to the State Department, Global Partnership funding has totaled $21 billion since 2002. The United States has promised an additional $10 billion in Global Partnership funds in the 2012-2022 timeframe, subject to congressional appropriations.

At the 2002 summit, G-8 countries adopted principles to deny terrorists access to WMD and WMD materials. These are:

- Strengthen multilateral treaties and other instruments to prevent WMD proliferation and strengthen the institutions established to implement such agreements;

- Develop and maintain measures that ensure that the production, use, storage, and transport of WMD materials is safe and secure and provide such assistance to countries lacking the ability to secure such materials;

- Ensure that WMD storage facilities are physically secure and provide assistance to states where facilities lack protection;

- Implement border controls, law enforcement efforts and international cooperation to detect and interdict attempts to smuggle WMD materials and items and provide assistance to countries that lack appropriate resources;

- Maintain export controls over items that could be used to develop weapons of mass destruction and missiles; and

- Work to manage and dispose of fissile materials stocks that are no longer required for defense purposes, destroy all chemical weapons, and "minimize" stockpiles of dangerous biological agents.

The Partnership is intended to span the range of U.S. nonproliferation programs, starting in the former Soviet Union. Russia identified chemical weapons destruction and dismantlement of decommissioned nuclear submarines as its top priority projects; the G-7 have additionally identified disposition of fissile materials and employing former weapon scientists as high-priority projects. However, rather than adopting a common approach, a common fund, or a multilateral implementation mechanism, projects are funded bilaterally under government-to-government agreements with Russia. The G8 Global Partnership Working Group provides an informal coordinating mechanism. Various sub-working groups concentrate on specific nonproliferation areas.

The G-8 states have invited others to participate and contribute to the initiative, as well as adopt the nonproliferation principles and guidelines to facilitate implementation. As of April 2014, there were 27 members of the Global Partnership: Canada, France, Germany, Italy, Japan, Russian Federation, United Kingdom, United States, Australia, Belgium, Czech Republic, Denmark, European Union, Finland, Ireland, Kazakhstan, Mexico, the Netherlands, New Zealand, Norway, Poland, Republic of Korea, Sweden, Switzerland, Ukraine, Hungary, and the Philippines.

The G-8 decided to extend the Global Partnership at their 2011 Summit in Deauville, France. They reaffirmed the goals set out at the 2010 Summit for future Global Partnership activities: nuclear and radiological security, bio-security, scientist engagement, and facilitation of the implementation of U.N. Security Council Resolution 1540. Due to concerns by some G-8 countries over budgetary constraints, no commitment on a pledge amount or end-date was agreed upon.

The United States held the G-8 presidency in 2012, and the Obama Administration continued its policy of actively promoting expansion of the Partnership to new geographical regions.[6] Mexico joined in December 2012, the first Latin American state to participate. The United States has also promoted greater attention to bio-security in the context of the Global Partnership. Under its 2012 chairmanship, it created a sub-working group on biological security to encourage and coordinate projects in this area.

The United Kingdom's 2013 presidency focused on increasing projects, expanding GP membership, strengthening information security, and implementing UN Security Council Resolution 1540. Russia holds the G-8 presidency in 2014, but the other members of the G-8 will boycott the planned meeting in Sochi, Russia, and instead meet as the G-7 in Belgium.[7] It is not clear yet what impact this will have on the Global Partnership activities in Russia, but most of those projects are winding down and no cancellations have been announced. Global Partnership cooperation amongst countries other than Russia is expected to continue.

For Further Reading

CRS Report R43143, *The Evolution of Cooperative Threat Reduction: Issues for Congress*, by Mary Beth D. Nikitin and Amy F. Woolf

---

Multilateral Nuclear Nonproliferation Activities

The International Nuclear Nonproliferation Regime

The United States is a leader of an international regime that attempts to limit the spread of nuclear weapons through treaties, export control coordination and enforcement, and U.N. Security Council resolutions. Recent challenges to the regime—notably North Korea's October 2006, 2009, and 2013 nuclear tests and Iran's continued defiance of international demands to halt uranium enrichment and cooperate fully with the IAEA—raise questions about and reinforce the importance of nonproliferation policy. Moreover, increased awareness of the need to keep sensitive materials and technologies out of terrorist hands has reinvigorated efforts to control not just nuclear weapons and weapons-usable materials, but also radioactive materials that could be used in radiological dispersal devices. Key issues in this area that the 113th Congress might consider include how the nuclear nonproliferation regime is affected by Iran's suspected weapons program; how to prevent Iran from developing nuclear weapons; North Korea's nuclear weapons activities; U.S. nuclear cooperation with India; tensions between India and Pakistan as amplified by their nuclear weapons programs; and a predicted expansion in civilian nuclear energy facilities worldwide that will challenge the safeguards regime. Congress may also consider how cooperation under the international nonproliferation regimes can be leveraged to prevent nuclear terrorism.

---

[6] "Global Partnership 2012," State Department website, http://www.state.gov/t/isn/c12743.htm.

[7] "G-7 Leaders Statement," The White House, March 2, 2014, http://www.whitehouse.gov/the-press-office/2014/03/02/g-7-leaders-statement.

The Nuclear Nonproliferation Treaty

The Nuclear Nonproliferation Treaty (NPT), which entered into force in 1970 and was extended indefinitely in 1995, is the centerpiece of the nuclear nonproliferation regime. The treaty currently has 190 States Parties. It is complemented by International Atomic Energy Agency (IAEA) safeguards, national export control laws, coordinated export control policies under the Nuclear Suppliers Group, U.N. Security Council resolutions, and ad hoc initiatives. The NPT recognizes five nations (the United States, Russia, France, Britain, and China) as nuclear weapon states—a distinction that is carried over in other parts of the regime and in national laws. Three nations that have not signed the NPT—India, Israel, and Pakistan—possess significant nuclear weapon capabilities. North Korea, which had signed the NPT but withdrew in 2003, is now thought to possess a small number of nuclear weapons. Several countries, including Argentina, Brazil, and South Africa, suspended their nuclear weapons programs and joined the NPT in the 1990s. Others—Ukraine, Belarus, and Kazakhstan—gave up former Soviet weapons on their territories and joined the NPT as non-nuclear weapon states in the 1990s.

The Nuclear Nonproliferation Treaty is unique in its near universality—only India, Pakistan, Israel, and North Korea are now outside the treaty. In signing the NPT, non-nuclear weapon states (NNWS) pledge not to acquire nuclear weapons in exchange for a pledge by the nuclear weapon states (NWS) not to assist the development of nuclear weapons by any NNWS and to facilitate "the fullest possible exchange of equipment, materials and scientific and technological information for the peaceful uses of nuclear energy." (NPT, Article IV-2) The NWS, defined as any state that tested a nuclear explosive before 1967, also agree to "pursue negotiations in good faith on effective measures relating to cessation of the nuclear arms race at an early date and to nuclear disarmament." (NPT, Article VI). Many NNWS have often expressed dissatisfaction with the apparent lack of progress toward disarmament.

Nuclear proliferation often has significant regional security repercussions, but there is also a growing realization that the current constellation of proliferation risks may require further improvements to the system itself. Concern has shifted from keeping technology from the states outside the NPT to stemming potential further proliferation, either from those states outside the regime or through black markets, such as the Pakistani A.Q. Khan network. Currently, member states of the NPT are grappling with ways to strengthen controls within the current system and through ad hoc complementary measures.

The International Atomic Energy Agency (IAEA)

The International Atomic Energy Agency was established in 1957 to assist nations in their peaceful nuclear programs (primarily research and nuclear power programs) and to safeguard nuclear materials from these peaceful programs to ensure that they are not diverted to nuclear weapons uses. The IAEA safeguards system relies on data collection, review, and periodic inspections at declared facilities. The IAEA may also inspect other facilities if it suspects undeclared nuclear materials or weapons-related activities are present.

Non-nuclear weapon NPT members are required to declare and submit all nuclear materials in their possession to regular IAEA inspections to ensure that sensitive nuclear materials and technologies are not diverted from civilian to military purposes. Some states who are not parties to the NPT (India, Israel, Pakistan) are members of the IAEA and allow inspections of some, but not all, of their nuclear activities. The IAEA also provides technical assistance for peaceful applications of nuclear technology for energy, medicine, agriculture, and research.

After the 1991 Persian Gulf War, IAEA inspection teams working with the U.N. Special Commission on Iraq (UNSCOM) revealed an extensive covert nuclear weapons program that had been virtually undetected by annual inspections of Baghdad's declared facilities. This knowledge inspired efforts to strengthen the IAEA's authority to conduct more intrusive inspections of a wider variety of installations, to provide the Agency with intelligence information about suspected covert nuclear activities, and to provide the Agency with the resources and political support needed to increase confidence in its safeguards system. In 1998, the IAEA adopted an "Additional Protocol" that would give the agency greater authority and access to verify nuclear declarations. The protocol enters into force for individual NPT states upon ratification. As of March 2014, 143 countries have signed an Additional Protocol and 122 have entered into force. The Senate gave its advice and consent to the protocol on March 31, 2004 (Treaty Doc. 107-7, Senate Executive Report 108-12). On December 18, 2006, implementing legislation was passed in P.L. 109-401, as part of the Hyde Act. On December 30, 2008, the President signed the instrument of ratification for the Additional Protocol. It was deposited with the IAEA and entered into force on January 6, 2009.

The IAEA has had an expanded mission in recent years, increasingly called upon to implement nuclear security-related activities. The IAEA also faces a potential worldwide expansion in the number of nuclear power plants it will need to monitor. Congress may consider U.S. support for the IAEA in light of these challenges. The Department of Energy's National Nuclear Security Administration is studying the future of international safeguards through its Next Generation Safeguards Initiative, which includes how to better share U.S. expertise and new safeguards technologies with the IAEA.

Nuclear-Weapon-Free Zones

Several regions of the world have treaties in force that ban the development, deployment, and use of nuclear weapons, known as nuclear-weapon-free zones, including Latin America (Treaty of Tlatelolco), Central Asia (Treaty on a Nuclear-Weapon-Free Zone in Central Asia), the South Pacific (Treaty of Rarotonga), Africa (Treaty of Pelindaba), and Southeast Asia (Treaty of Bangkok). Mongolia has declared itself a single-state Nuclear-Weapon-Free Zone. Also, the Treaty of Antarctica established that Antarctica will be used for peaceful uses only. Nuclear weapons are also banned on the seabed, in outer space, and on the moon by international treaties.

The nuclear-weapon-free zones (NWFZs) reinforce the undertakings of NPT non-nuclear-weapon state members and give confidence at a regional level that states are not seeking nuclear weapons. Each treaty has protocols for nuclear weapon states to ratify. These protocols are pledges that the nuclear weapon states will not base nuclear weapons in the zone, test nuclear weapons in the zone, or use or threaten to use nuclear weapons against the countries in the zone. The "negative security assurance" provided to members of the zone through the nuclear weapon state protocol is considered one of the key benefits of membership for non-nuclear weapon states.

The United States ratified the protocols to the Latin American NWFZ. The Obama Administration, as pledged at the 2010 NPT Review Conference, submitted the Protocols to the Treaties of Pelindaba (Africa) and Rarotonga (South Pacific) to the Senate for advice and consent for ratification on May 2, 2011. The United States signed the protocols at the time these treaties were open for signature (April 11, 1996, for the Treaty of Pelindaba and August 6, 1985, for the Treaty of Rarotonga). The other four nuclear weapon states besides the United States (China, France, Russia, United Kingdom) have ratified those protocols.

The Obama Administration has also said it would work with parties to the Southeast Asian Nuclear-Weapon-Free Zone and the Central Asian Nuclear-Weapon-Free Zone to resolve outstanding issues related to the protocols in order to "sign the protocols to those treaties as soon as possible."[8] In August 2011, the United States along with the other four NPT nuclear weapon states began consultations with the SEANWFZ countries regarding the NWS protocols to that agreement. Those consultations reportedly continue. The five nuclear-weapon states announced their signature of the CANWFZ Protocol at the NPT Preparatory Committee meeting in May 2014.[9]

The five nuclear weapon states recognized Mongolia as a single-state nuclear-weapon-free zone in September 2012 by signing parallel declarations formally acknowledging this status.[10]

Talks are underway to discuss the establishment of a Middle East WMD-free zone.

Table 1. U.S. Adherence to Nuclear-Weapon-Free Zone Protocols

	Year Treaty Opened for Signature/Entered into Force	Year United States Signed Protocols	Year United States Ratified Protocols
Treaty of Tlatelolco (Latin America)	1967/1969	Protocol I: 1977 Protocol II: 1968	Protocol I: 1981 Protocol II: 1971
Treaty on a Nuclear-Weapon-Free Zone in Central Asia	2006/2009	5/6/14	Not ratified
Treaty of Rarotonga (South Pacific)	1985/1986	Protocol I, II & III: 1996	Not ratified, submitted to the Senate, May 2, 2011
Treaty of Pelindaba (Africa)	1996/2009	Protocols I & II: 1996	Not ratified, submitted to the Senate, May 2, 2011
Treaty of Bangkok (Southeast Asia)	1995/1997	Not signed	Not ratified

Nuclear Suppliers Group

The United States has been a leader in establishing export controls, a key component of the nuclear nonproliferation regime. The Atomic Energy Act of 1954 and Nuclear Nonproliferation Act of 1978 established controls on nuclear exports that gradually gained acceptance by other nuclear suppliers. The Export Administration Act of 1979 (EAA) authorized controls on dual-use technology that could contribute to foreign weapons. Export controls require exporters to get a license before selling sensitive technology to foreign buyers and, in some cases, ban certain exports to some countries.

International nuclear controls are coordinated by an informal association of 46 nuclear exporters called the Nuclear Suppliers Group (NSG), founded in 1975. NSG members voluntarily agree to

---

[8] "Statement on Nuclear-Free Zones in Asia and Africa," White House Press Release, May 2, 2011. http://www.whitehouse.gov/the-press-office/2011/05/02/statement-nuclear-free-zones-asia-and-africa.

[9] http://www.state.gov/r/pa/prs/ps/2014/05/225681 htm.

[10] Daryl G. Kimball, "Mongolia Recognized as Nuclear-Free Zone," *Arms Control Today*, September/October 2012.

coordinate exports of civilian nuclear material and nuclear-related equipment and technology to non-nuclear weapon states. The Group agreed to guidelines for export that include lists of materials and equipment that are to be subject to export control. NSG guidelines require that the recipient country offer assurances that the importing items will not be used for a weapons program, will have proper physical security, and will not be transferred to a third party without the permission of the exporter. Recipient countries' nuclear program must also have full-scope IAEA safeguards. In September 2008, the NSG agreed to exempt India from the full-scope safeguards requirement, although retained a policy of restraint on the transfer enrichment and reprocessing equipment. NSG members in June 2011 adopted additional guidelines that define eligibility criteria for the transfer of enrichment and reprocessing technologies to new states.

The NSG's effectiveness is limited by its voluntary nature and, therefore, lack of verification or enforcement mechanisms. Countries such as Iraq and Pakistan, and individuals like A.Q. Khan and others have exploited weaknesses in the national export control systems of many countries to acquire a wide range of nuclear items.

Convention on the Physical Protection of Nuclear Material

The Convention on the Physical Protection of Nuclear Material, adopted in 1987, sets international standards for nuclear trade and commerce. The Convention established security requirements for the protection of nuclear materials against terrorism; parties to the treaty agree to report to the IAEA on the disposition of nuclear materials being transported and agree to provide appropriate security during such transport. As of April 2014, 149 countries were party to the treaty and 44 were signatories.

The United States had advocated strengthening the treaty by extending controls to domestic facility security, not just transportation. In July 2005, States Parties convened to extend the Convention's scope to cover not only nuclear material in international transport, but also nuclear material in domestic use, storage, and transport, as well as the protection of nuclear material and facilities from sabotage. The new rules will come into effect once they have been ratified by two-thirds of the States Parties of the Convention, which could take several years. As of April 2014, 74 states had deposited their instruments of ratification, acceptance, or approval of the amendment with the depositary. The United States has not yet submitted its instrument of ratification.

The United States has not yet submitted its instrument of ratification to the Convention. On September 4, 2007, President Bush submitted the amendment to the Senate for its advice and consent on ratification. The Senate Committee on Foreign Relations recommended that the Senate give its advice and consent on September 11, 2008. The Senate must also approve implementing legislation before the United States deposits its instrument of ratification to the Amendment. In the 112th Congress, the Obama Administration submitted draft legislation to the Senate Judiciary Committee in April 2011. The House passed implementing legislation in the 112th Congress, but the Senate did not take action. In the 113th Congress, the House passed the Nuclear Terrorism Conventions Implementation and Safety of Maritime Navigation Act of 2013 (H.R. 1073) in May 2013, which approved implementing legislation for the CPPNM Amendment and the Nuclear Terrorism Convention (as well as agreements on maritime security). The Senate has not taken action.

For Further Reading

CRS Report RL31559, *Proliferation Control Regimes: Background and Status*, coordinated by Mary Beth D. Nikitin

CRS Report R41216, *2010 Non-Proliferation Treaty (NPT) Review Conference: Key Issues and Implications*, coordinated by Paul K. Kerr and Mary Beth D. Nikitin

CRS Report RL34234, *Managing the Nuclear Fuel Cycle: Policy Implications of Expanding Global Access to Nuclear Power*, coordinated by Mary Beth D. Nikitin

CRS Report RL33016, *U.S. Nuclear Cooperation with India: Issues for Congress*, by Paul K. Kerr

International Convention for the Suppression of Acts of Nuclear Terrorism

The U.N. General Assembly adopted the International Convention for the Suppression of Acts of Nuclear Terrorism (also known as the Nuclear Terrorism Convention) in 2005 after eight years of debating a draft treaty proposed by Russia in 1997.[11] Disputes over the definition of terrorism, omitted in the final version, and over the issue of nuclear weapons use by states, complicated the discussions for many years. After September 11, 2001, states revisited the draft treaty and the necessary compromises were made. The Convention entered into force in July 2007. There were 83 states parties and 115 signatories as of February 2013.

The United States has strongly supported the Convention, and President Bush was the second to sign it (after Russian President Putin) on September 14, 2005. The Senate Committee on Foreign Relations reported the treaty to the full Senate and recommended advice and consent on September 11, 2008. The Senate must approve implementing legislation before the United States deposits its instrument of ratification to the Convention. In the 112th Congress, the Obama Administration submitted draft legislation to the Senate Judiciary Committee in April 2011. The House passed implementing legislation in the 112th Congress, but the Senate did not take action. In the 113th Congress, the House passed the Nuclear Terrorism Conventions Implementation and Safety of Maritime Navigation Act of 2013 (H.R. 1073) in May 2013, which approved implementing legislation for the CPPNM Amendment and the Nuclear Terrorism Convention (as well as agreements on maritime security). The Senate has not taken action.

The Convention defines offenses related to the unlawful possession and use of radioactive or nuclear material or devices, and the use or damage to nuclear facilities. The Convention commits each party to adopt measures in its national law to criminalize these offenses and make them punishable. It covers acts by individuals, not states, and does not govern the actions of armed forces during an armed conflict. The Convention also does not address "the issue of legality of the use or threat of use of nuclear weapons by States." It also commits States Parties to exchange information and cooperate to "detect, prevent, suppress and investigate" those suspected of committing nuclear terrorism, including extraditions.

For Further Reading

CRS Report RL32595, *Nuclear Terrorism: A Brief Review of Threats and Responses*, by Jonathan E. Medalia

CRS Report R41169, *Securing Nuclear Materials: The 2012 Summit and Issues for Congress*, by Mary Beth D. Nikitin

---

[11] See full text at http://untreaty.un.org/English/Terrorism/English_18_15.pdf.

Comprehensive Test Ban Treaty[12]

The Comprehensive Test Ban Treaty (CTBT) would ban all nuclear explosions. It opened for signature in 1996 but has not yet entered into force. Previous treaties have restricted nuclear testing: the 1963 Limited Test Ban Treaty barred explosions in the atmosphere, in space, and under water, and the 1974 U.S.-U.S.S.R. Threshold Test Ban Treaty and the 1976 Peaceful Nuclear Explosions Treaty limited the explosive yield of underground nuclear explosions. In the debate on the indefinite extension of the NPT in 1995, many non-nuclear weapon states saw the early conclusion of the CTBT as a key step by the nuclear weapon states to comply with their obligations under Article VI of the NPT; critics argue that the United States has taken many steps in support of these obligations. President Clinton signed the CTBT when it opened for signature and submitted the treaty to the Senate for advice and consent in 1997. The Senate rejected the treaty by a vote of 48 for, 51 against, and 1 present, on October 13, 1999.

Parties to the treaty agree "not to carry out any nuclear weapon test explosion or any other nuclear explosion." The treaty establishes a Comprehensive Nuclear-Test-Ban Treaty Organization (CTBTO) of all member states to implement the treaty. The CTBTO oversees a Conference of States Parties, an Executive Council, and a Provisional Technical Secretariat. The latter would operate an International Data Center to process and report on data from an International Monitoring System (IMS), a global network that, when completed, would consist of 321 monitoring stations and 16 laboratories. A Protocol details the monitoring system and inspection procedures. The CTBTO would come into effect if the treaty entered into force; until that time, the CTBTO Preparatory Commission conducts work to prepare for entry into force, such as building and operating the IMS.

For the treaty to enter into force, 44 specified states must ratify it. As of April 1, 2014, 183 nations had signed the CTBT and 162 had ratified. Of the 44 required nations, 36 have ratified, 3 have not signed (India, North Korea, and Pakistan) and another 5 have not ratified (China, Egypt, Iran, Israel, and the United States). States that have ratified the treaty have held conferences every two years since 1999 to discuss how to accelerate entry into force.

The CTBT remains on the calendar of the Senate Foreign Relations Committee. The Bush Administration opposed U.S. ratification of the CTBT but continued a U.S. nuclear test moratorium in effect since October 1992. In contrast, President Obama has repeatedly stated his support for the CTBT. For example, he said, "As president, I will reach out to the Senate to secure the ratification of the CTBT at the earliest practical date and will then launch a diplomatic effort to bring onboard other states whose ratifications are required for the treaty to enter into force." Senator Hillary Clinton, as nominee for Secretary of State, previewed the Administration's approach to securing the Senate's advice and consent: "A lesson learned from [the treaty's defeat in] 1999 is that we need to ensure that the administration work intensively with Senators so they are fully briefed on key technical issues on which their CTBT votes will depend.... Substantial progress has been made in the last decade in our ability to verify a CTBT and ensure stockpile reliability." Critics respond that confidence in the nuclear stockpile requires nuclear testing, and that certain techniques would enable a determined cheater to avoid detection or attribution of its tests.

---

[12] For further details, contact Jonathan Medalia, CRS Specialist in National Defense, 7-7632.

Fissile Material Production Cutoff Treaty (FMCT)

The United States first proposed that the international community negotiate a ban on the production of fissile material (plutonium and enriched uranium) that could be used in nuclear weapons over 50 years ago. Negotiators of the NPT realized that fissile material usable for nuclear weapons could still be produced under the guise of peaceful nuclear activities within the Treaty. Consequently, a fissile material production ban, or FMCT, has remained on the long-term negotiating agenda at the Conference on Disarmament (CD) in Geneva. These negotiations have been largely stalled since 1993. In 1995, the CD agreed to the "Shannon Mandate," which called for an "non-discriminatory, multilateral and internationally and effectively verifiable treaty banning the production of fissile material for nuclear weapons or other nuclear explosive devices."

The Bush Administration undertook a comprehensive review of the U.S. position on the FMCT in 2004 and concluded that such a ban would be useful in creating "an observed norm against the production of fissile material intended for weapons," but argued that such a ban is inherently unverifiable. The Bush Administration proposed a draft treaty in May 2006 that contained no verification measures.

In contrast, the Obama Administration supports the negotiation of an FMCT with verification measures on the basis of the Shannon mandate. President Obama said in an April 2009 speech that "to cut off the building blocks needed for a bomb, the United States will seek a new treaty that verifiably ends the production of fissile materials intended for use in state nuclear weapons. If we are serious about stopping the spread of these weapons, then we should put an end to the dedicated production of weapons-grade materials that create them." One key issue is whether or not such a treaty would seek to include existing stocks of fissile material. The United States has strongly objected to such an approach, but it is supported by some non-nuclear weapon states.[13]

Substantively, it has always been important to capture the undeclared nuclear weapon states (initially India, Pakistan, and Israel, but now also North Korea) that were not parties to the NPT and therefore subject to very few if any restrictions or monitoring. Many observers believed that negotiations at the CD were preferable to smaller, eight-party talks (United States, United Kingdom, France, China, Russia, India, Pakistan, and Israel) because they would establish a global norm and would not have the appearance of conferring nuclear weapons status upon India, Pakistan, and Israel. As of April 1, 2014, negotiations in the Conference on Disarmament have not begun, with Pakistan blocking any forward movement (the CD operates on the basis of consensus). U.S. Assistant Secretary of State Rose Gottemoeller said in an opening statement to the CD in January 2011 that while the United States views the CD as the appropriate forum for

---

[13] The states advocating inclusion of stocks refer to such a treaty as the Fissile Material Treaty (FMT).

FMCT negotiations, other options should be considered if the stalemate continues.[14] In 2011, Japan and Australia hosted technical consultations on the margins of the CD. The United States initiated P-5 consultations on verification aspects of a possible treaty, and these meetings continue.

Although negotiations have not yet begun, it could be important to begin a public debate through hearings on various options and approaches to end the production of fissile material for weapons. Some outcomes, particularly those that include intrusive verification, could have an impact on U.S. facilities that are not currently being monitored. Another aspect for congressional consideration is how well-equipped the U.S. intelligence community is to verify any such agreement, and what the role of the International Atomic Energy Agency (IAEA) should be.

For Further Reading

CRS Report RS22474, *Banning Fissile Material Production for Nuclear Weapons: Prospects for a Treaty (FMCT)*, by Sharon Squassoni

CRS Report RL31559, *Proliferation Control Regimes: Background and Status*, coordinated by Mary Beth D. Nikitin

---

Informal Cooperative Endeavors

Global Threat Reduction Initiative

On May 26, 2004, Secretary of Energy Spencer Abraham announced the Global Threat Reduction Initiative (GTRI). GTRI has consolidated and accelerated several programs the Department of Energy was already conducting:

- Russian Research Reactor Fuel Return (RRRFR) program (to repatriate all fresh and spent Russian-origin nuclear fuel residing at reactors around the world);

- Reduced Enrichment for Research and Test Reactors (RERTR) program (to convert the cores of 105 civilian research reactors that use high-enriched uranium (HEU) to low-enriched uranium (LEU));

- Foreign Research Reactor Spent Nuclear Fuel (FRRSNF) Acceptance program (to accelerate and complete the repatriation of U.S.-origin research reactor spent HEU fuel (about 20 metric tons from more than 40 locations worldwide));

- U.S. and International Radiological Threat Reduction (USRTR and IRTR) programs (to identify, recover and store domestic radioactive sealed sources and other radiological materials and reduce the international threat posed by radiological materials that could be used in "dirty bombs.")

A new program added to the mix is the Global Research Reactor Security Program, which provides security upgrades to research reactor facilities that store highly enriched uranium (HEU) that could be used to develop a nuclear weapon. The Kazakhstan Spent Fuel program provides security for long-term storage of nearly 3 tons of weapons-grade plutonium and 10 tons of HEU in spent fuel. In September 2004, the United States and Russia convened a GTRI International

---

[14] Assistant Secretary of State Rose Gottemoeller, "2011 Opening Statement to the Conference on Disarmament," January 27, 2011.

Partners' Conference to build support for GTRI-related projects. Reportedly, over 90 countries joined GTRI after its inception, promising to spend about $450 million over the next decade.

Proliferation Security Initiative (PSI)

President Bush announced the Proliferation Security Initiative (PSI) on May 31, 2003. This Initiative is primarily a diplomatic tool developed by the United States to gain support for interdicting shipments of weapons of mass destruction-related (WMD) equipment and materials. Through the PSI, the Bush Administration sought to "create a web of counterproliferation partnerships through which proliferators will have difficulty carrying out their trade in WMD and missile-related technology." The states involved in PSI have agreed to review their national legal authorities for interdiction, provide consent for other states to board and search their own flag vessels, and conclude ship-boarding agreements. The Proliferation Security Initiative has no budget, no formal offices supporting it, no international secretariat, and no formal mechanism for measuring its effectiveness (like a database of cases). To many, these attributes are positive, allowing the United States to respond swiftly to changing developments. Others question whether the international community can sustain this effort over the longer term. The Obama Administration officials have pledged to "institutionalize" PSI, although how they will carry this out is not yet clear.

As of April 1, 2014, over 100 countries have committed formally to PSI participation. Sixteen "core" nations have pledged their cooperation in interdicting shipments of WMD materials, agreeing in Paris in 2003 on a set of interdiction principles. The 9/11 Commission Act of 2007 recommended that PSI be expanded and coordination within the U.S. government improved. The United States has prioritized the conclusion of ship-boarding agreements with key states that have high volumes of international shipping. So far, the United States has signed 11 agreements with Antigua and Barbuda, the Bahamas, Belize, Croatia, Cyprus, Liberia, Malta, the Marshall Islands, Mongolia, Panama, and Saint Vincent and the Grenadines.

Since PSI is an activity rather than an organization, and has no budget or internal U.S. government organization, it may be difficult for Congress to track PSI's progress. Several intelligence resource issues may be of interest to Congress, including whether intelligence information is good enough for effective implementation and whether intelligence-sharing requirements have been established with non-NATO allies. Another issue may be how PSI is coordinated with other federal interdiction-related programs, like export control assistance. Reporting and coordination requirements now in public law may result in more information and better interagency coordination than in the past.

For Further Reading

CRS Report RL34327, *Proliferation Security Initiative (PSI)*, by Mary Beth D. Nikitin

---

United Nations Security Council Resolution 1540

In April 2004, the U.N. Security Council adopted Resolution 1540, which requires all states to "criminalize proliferation, enact strict export controls and secure all sensitive materials within their borders." UNSCR 1540 called on states to enforce effective domestic controls over WMD and WMD-related materials in production, use, storage, and transport; to maintain effective border controls, and to develop national export and trans-shipment controls over such items, all of which should help interdiction efforts. The resolution did not, however, provide any enforcement authority, nor did it specifically mention interdiction. About two-thirds of all states have reported to the U.N. on their efforts to strengthen defenses against WMD trafficking. U.N. Security Council Resolutions 1673 (2006), 1810 (2008), and 1977 (2011) extended the duration of the 1540 Committee. The 2011 resolution extended the committee's mandate for 10 years. The committee is currently focused on identifying assistance projects for states in need and matching donors to improve these WMD controls. Congress may consider how the U.S. is contributing to this international effort.

Global Initiative to Combat Nuclear Terrorism

In July 2006, Russia and the United States announced the creation of the Global Initiative to Combat Nuclear Terrorism before the G-8 Summit in St. Petersburg. Like PSI, this initiative is nonbinding, and requires agreement on a statement of principles. Thirteen nations—Australia, Canada, China, France, Germany, Italy, Japan, Kazakhstan, Morocco, Turkey, the United Kingdom, the United States, and Russia—endorsed a Statement of Principles at the Initiative's first meeting in October 2006.[15] The International Atomic Energy Agency (IAEA) and the European Union (EU) have observer status. As of April 2014, 85 states have agreed to the statement of principles and are Global Initiative partner nations.[16]

U.S. officials have described the Initiative as a "flexible framework" to prevent, detect, and respond to the threat of nuclear terrorism. It is meant to enhance information sharing and build capacity worldwide. The Statement of Principles pledges to improve each nation's ability to secure radioactive and nuclear material, prevent illicit trafficking by improving detection of such material, respond to a terrorist attack, prevent safe haven to potential nuclear terrorists and financial resources, and ensure liability for acts of nuclear terrorism. Participating states share a common goal to improve national capabilities to combat nuclear terrorism by sharing best practices through multinational exercises and expert level meetings. Without dues or a secretariat, actions under the Initiative will take legal guidance from the International Convention on the Suppression of Acts of Nuclear Terrorism, the Convention on the Physical Protection of Nuclear Materials and U.N. Security Council Resolutions 1540 and 1373.[17]

Global Initiative partner nations periodically hold exercises and workshops to improve coordination and exchange best practices. These are the primary activities held under the initiative.[18] The Global Initiative does not have program funding of its own in the U.S. budget, and therefore Congress may consider whether its goals can be achieved within these constraints.

Ad Hoc Sanctions and Incentives

Other efforts—such as economic, military, or security assistance—may also help slow the proliferation of nuclear weapons. These cooperative measures have been effective in some cases (South Korea, Taiwan, Belarus, Kazakhstan, Ukraine), but failed in others (Iraq, Israel, Pakistan).

---

[15] "Partner Nations Endorse Global Initiative to Combat Nuclear Terrorism Statement of Principles," U.S. Department of State, Bureau of International Security and Nonproliferation, November 7, 2006.

[16] Current list may be viewed at http://www.state.gov/t/isn/c37083.htm.

[17] "U.S.-Russia Joint Fact Sheet on The Global Initiative to Combat Nuclear Terrorism," July 15, 2006. http://www.state.gov/r/pa/prs/ps/2006/69016 htm.

[18] For a full list, see http://www.state.gov/documents/organization/145498.pdf.

Some favor greater use of sanctions against countries that violate international nonproliferation standards, while others view sanctions as self-defeating. Most observers conclude that a mix of positive and negative incentives, including diplomacy to address underlying regional security problems, provides the best opportunity for controlling the spread of nuclear weapons. However, when diplomacy fails, some policy-makers have argued that military measures may be necessary to attack nuclear and other weapons of mass destruction and related facilities in states hostile to the United States or its allies. For example, the Bush Administration claimed that the overthrow of the Saddam Hussein regime in Iraq was justified, in part, on the basis of claims that Iraq possessed chemical and biological weapons and might resume efforts to develop nuclear weapons. As developments revealed, however, accurate intelligence is a key component of both diplomatic and military approaches to nonproliferation.

Non-Nuclear Multilateral Endeavors

The international community has concluded a number of arms control agreements, conventions, and arrangements that affect non-nuclear weapons. Two of these, the Conventional Armed Forces in Europe Treaty (CFE) and the Open Skies Treaty were a part of the late-Cold War effort to enhance stability and predictability in Europe. Others seek to control the spread of technologies that might contribute to developing conventional or unconventional weapons programs. Finally, several seek to ban whole classes of weapons through international conventions.

European Conventional Arms Control

Conventional Armed Forces in Europe Treaty (CFE)

In late 1990, 22 members of NATO and the Warsaw Pact signed the Conventional Armed Forces in Europe (CFE) Treaty, agreeing to limit NATO and Warsaw Pact non-nuclear forces in an area from the Atlantic Ocean to the Ural Mountains. The CFE treaty did not anticipate the dissolution of the Soviet Union and the Warsaw Pact. Consequently, the participants signed the so-called "Tashkent Agreement" in May 1992, allocating responsibility for the Soviet Union's Treaty-Limited items of Equipment (TLEs) among Azerbaijan, Armenia, Belarus, Kazakhstan, Moldova, Russia, Ukraine, and Georgia. It also established equipment ceilings for each nation and the implied responsibility for the destruction/transfer of equipment necessary to meet these national ceilings. In 1999, the CFE Adaptation Agreement was signed to further adjust to the dissolution of the Warsaw Pact and the expansion of NATO. As discussed below, this agreement has not entered into force pending its ratification by NATO members, and Russia has suspended its participation in the CFE Treaty.

Key Limits and Restrictions

CFE placed alliance-wide, regional (zonal), and national ceilings on specific major items of military equipment.[19] It sought to promote stability not only by reducing armaments, but also by

---

[19] The Treaty limits battle tanks, artillery, armored combat vehicles, attack helicopters, and combat aircraft. Other types of equipment are subject to operating restrictions and reporting requirements: primary trainer aircraft, unarmed trainer aircraft, combat support helicopters, unarmed transport helicopters, armored vehicle-launched bridges, armored personnel carrier "look-alikes" and armored combat vehicle "look-alikes."

reducing the possibility of surprise attack by preventing large concentrations of forces. The CFE treaty also provides for (1) very detailed data exchanges on equipment, force structure, and training maneuvers; (2) specific procedures for the destruction or redistribution of excess equipment; and (3) verification of compliance through on-site inspections. Its implementation has resulted in an unprecedented reduction of conventional arms in Europe, with over 50,000 (TLEs) removed or destroyed; almost all agree it has achieved most of its initial objectives.

Under the CFE treaty all equipment reductions needed to comply with overall, national, and zonal ceilings were to have been completed by November 1995. As this deadline approached, it was evident that Russia would not meet those requirements, particularly in the so-called "flank zones," which include the Leningrad Military District in the north, and more importantly, the North Caucasus Military District in the south. The outbreak of armed ethnic conflicts in and around the Caucasus, most notably in Chechnya, led Russia to claim it needed to deploy equipment in excess of treaty limits in that zone. Russia placed this claim in the context of broader assertions that some CFE provisions reflected Cold War assumptions and did not fairly address its new national security concerns. Further, it argued that economic hardship was making the movement of forces unaffordable in some cases.

To address these concerns, the CFE parties negotiated a Flank Agreement, in early 1996. This Agreement removed several Russian (and one Ukrainian) administrative districts from the old "flank zone," thus permitting existing flank equipment ceilings to apply to a smaller area. To provide some counterbalance to these adjustments, reporting requirements were enhanced, inspection rights in the zone increased, and district ceilings were placed on armored combat vehicles to prevent their concentration.

The Adaptation Agreement

The 1996 CFE Review Conference opened negotiations to modify the treaty to account for the absence of the USSR and the Warsaw Pact, and the expansion of NATO into the Czech Republic, Poland, and Hungary. Most CFE signatories did not want to completely renegotiate the treaty. Russia, however, sought broader revisions, and, ironically, it sought to maintain the alliance-wide equipment ceilings. An alliance-wide cap on NATO would presumably force adjustments of national holdings as the NATO alliance expanded; such adjustments probably would *not* favor new member nations close to Russia's borders. The CFE parties did not adopt Russia's position and Russia ultimately agreed to a largely NATO-drafted document. This agreement called for, among other things, lower equipment levels throughout the "Atlantic to the Urals" area; enhanced verification procedures; and the replacement of NATO-Warsaw Pact "bloc to bloc" ceilings with national limits on all categories of TLEs. It also stated that the Flank Agreement was to remain in effect. The Adaptation Agreement reiterates that NATO has "no plan, no intention, and no reason" to deploy nuclear weapons on new members' territory; and seeks to improve new members' defensive capabilities through interoperability and capability for reinforcement, rather than by stationing additional combat forces on new members' territory. Russia's most serious focus has been, however, on NATO enlargement and how CFE could adapt to mitigate what many Russians see as an encroaching threat. Russia has called for the new members of NATO, particularly the Baltic states of Latvia, Lithuania, and Estonia, to become CFE state parties. These countries have indicated a willingness to join, however, they cannot do so until the Adaptation Agreement is ratified and the new CFE regime comes into force.

At the Istanbul Summit in 1999, where the Adaptation Agreement was concluded, Russia undertook the so-called Istanbul Commitments to remove its troops from both the Republic of

Georgia and the "breakaway" province of Transdniestra in Moldova.[20] Though not part of the CFE Adaptation Agreement document, NATO members have considered Russian fulfillment of these commitments a prerequisite for the ratification of the Agreement. Consequently, of the CFE signatories only Russia, Belarus, Ukraine, and Kazakhstan ratified the adapted treaty.

Compliance Concerns

In past compliance reports, the State Department has asserted that Russian equipment holdings "continue to exceed most of the legally binding limits for both the original and revised flank zones."[21] It also cited Russia for relatively minor reporting violations and for its failure to complete withdrawals of its troops from Georgia and Moldova. It also cited Armenia, Azerbaijan, Belarus, and Ukraine for noncompliance.[22] Armenia and Azerbaijan, engaged in a conflict over the Nagorno-Karabakh territory, have not completed equipment reductions; nor provided complete equipment declarations; nor provided timely notification of new equipment acquisition. Belarus was also cited for questionable equipment declarations and its refusal to allow inspectors access to an equipment storage site. The State Department deems Ukraine to have substantially complied with CFE requirements, but notes that it retained several hundred equipment items in excess of treaty limits. The State Department has raised significant issues with Russia's compliance, particularly in the years since Russia suspended its participation in the treaty.

Russian CFE Suspension

On April 26, 2007, Russian President Putin announced a "moratorium" on Russian CFE compliance, pointing to, among other things, the NATO nations' not having ratified the treaty as adapted. Subsequently, in statements to the press and diplomatic conferences, Russian officials elucidated the Russian position and its concerns. Among the major points are the following:[23]

- During its CFE "moratorium" Russia will not allow CFE inspections nor will it report on its military movements.

- The Istanbul Commitments regarding troop withdrawals in Georgia and Moldova are not an integral part of the CFE Adaptation Agreement document, and consequently not legally binding and should not stand in the way of NATO members' ratification of the Agreement.

- The Baltic States and Slovakia are not bound by the CFE and their NATO membership, coupled with the new U.S. basing agreements with Poland, Bulgaria, and Romania, constitute an unacceptable encroachment on Russian national security.

---

[20] For more information concerning the Georgian and Moldovan negotiations with Russia over its troop deployments in their countries, see CRS Report RS21981, *Moldova: Background and U.S. Policy*, by Steven Woehrel, and CRS Report RL33453, *Armenia, Azerbaijan, and Georgia: Political Developments and Implications for U.S. Interests*, by Jim Nichol and Steven Woehrel.

[21] *Adherence to and Compliance with Arms Control and Nonproliferation Agreements and Commitments.* Department of State, 2005 p. 47. The State Department did not publish this statutorily-mandated report to Congress in 2006.

[22] Ibid., pp. 16-28.

[23] "Russia May Withdraw from Agreement with NATO", *RIA Novosti*, April 27, 2007; "Russian Paper Examines NATO Ties, Impact of CFE Moratorium," BBC Monitoring Service May 1, 2007. Translation from *Kommersant*, April 28, 2007.

- If the NATO nations do not ratify the CFE Adaptation Agreement within a year, Russia will consider complete withdrawal from the treaty.

Russian officials, military leaders, and political commentators increasingly referred to the CFE treaty as a "Cold War agreement," which no longer reflected the realities of the European security environment. Russian military officials' consultations at NATO Headquarters on May 10 brought no softening of the Russian position. A Russian request to the Organization for Security and Cooperation in Europe for a special conference of CFE signatories in June was granted.[24] The conference failed to resolve any of the outstanding issues, and the State Parties were unable to find sufficient common ground to issue a final joint statement.

The European and U.S. governments reacted with some surprise at the harshness of Russian statements, and urged Russia to address its concerns within the consultative framework of the treaty rather than pursue a withdrawal. However, then-Secretary of State Rice and Secretary of Defense Gates, in conversations with President Putin and Russian Foreign Minister Lavrov, and Assistant Secretary of State for European and Eurasian Affairs in testimony before the U.S. Commission on Security and Cooperation in Europe, reiterated the U.S. position that ratification of the CFE Adaptation Agreement still remained contingent upon Russia fulfilling its commitment to withdraw its military forces from Georgia and Moldova.[25]

On November 30, 2007, President Putin signed legislation from the Duma that suspended Russian compliance with CFE, effective December 12, 2007. This action came during the Madrid OSCE summit meeting and evoked an expression of regret on the part of NATO officials, who noted that Russia's military posture would be under discussion at the NATO foreign ministers meeting in December. Undersecretary of State Nicholas Burns characterized the Russian action as a "mistake" and urged Russia to negotiate its concerns within the CFE framework. Russian officials emphasized that this action was not a withdrawal from the treaty, and that they were willing to participate in further discussions if they perceived a greater willingness on the part of the NATO allies to address their concerns. However, in recent years, it has become clear that Russia does not intend to return to the CFE Treaty; it would prefer the negotiation of a new agreement that reflected the new security environment in Europe.

Russian officials indicated, in 2007, that Russia did not plan to conduct any significant redeployment of forces outside the treaty limits. However, in August 2008, Russia sent military forces into Georgia without the consent of the Georgian government and recognized two provinces of Georgia, Abkhazia and South Ossetia, as independent states. U.S. officials have noted that these steps are inconsistent with Russia's obligation under the CFE Treaty to "to refrain ... from the threat or use of force against the territorial integrity or political independence of any State." In addition, because Russia has suspended its participation in the treaty, it has not allowed any on-site inspections and has not provided any data mandated by the treaty.

Some observers, and Russian spokesmen, have portrayed the Russian moves regarding CFE as an asymmetrical response to the proposed deployment of a U.S. ground-based missile defense system in Poland and the Czech Republic.[26] Others, including Chief of the Russian General Staff

---

[24] "Russian MP Says New Structure of European Security on the Agenda," *ITAR-TASS World Service*, May 11, 2007.

[25] Transcript of Secretary of State Rice Media Availability, Moscow, May 15, 2007. Federal Document Clearing House; Transcript of Hearing before the U.S. Commission on Security and Cooperation in Europe, May 24, 2007. Federal Document Clearing House.

[26] "U.S. and NATO Dissect Putin Treaty Threat," *Financial Times*, April 27, 2007 p. 2.

Baluyevsky, have discounted a specific linkage, seeing the missile defense controversy as merely one element of a more broadly ranged dissatisfaction with changes in the European security environment, which, from the Russian perspective, have favored the NATO allies.[27]

Legislation was introduced in both the House and Senate, during the 110th Congress (H.Res. 603, S.Res. 278), characterizing the Russian actions as "regrettable," and urging the Russian Federation to reconsider its intentions and to fulfill the Istanbul Commitments, while encouraging all CFE State Parties to seek "innovative and constructive" mechanisms to resolves these issues. S.Res. 278 passed the Senate by unanimous consent, while H.Res. 603 was never reported out by the House Foreign Affairs Committee.

The U.S. Response

In November 2011, the United States announced that it would stop implementing its data exchange obligations under the CFE Treaty with respect to Russia. The United States would continue to share data with other treaty partners, and would not exceed the numerical limits on conventional armaments and equipment established by the treaty. But it would withhold data from Russia because Russia has refused to accept inspections and ceased to provide information to other CFE Treaty parties since its 2007 decision.

The U.S. State Department, in its statement on the treaty, indicated that the United States remained committed to revitalizing conventional arms control in Europe. It also indicated that, in order to increase transparency and promote stability in the region, the United States would voluntarily inform Russia of any significant change in the U.S. force posture in Europe.

For Further Reading

Treaty on Conventional Armed Forces in Europe. http://www.state.gov/t/ac/trt/4781.htm.

Adherence to and Compliance with Arms Control and Nonproliferation Agreements and Commitments. Department of State, 2005.

CRS Report 90-615 RCO, *Treaty of Conventional Armed Forces in Europe (CFE): A Primer.* (Out of print. For copies contact Amy Woolf, 7-23790.)

Treaty on Open Skies[28]

On March 24, 1992, the United States, Canada, and 22 European nations signed the Treaty on Open Skies. The parties agreed to permit unarmed aircraft to conduct observation flights over their territories. Although the flights will likely focus on military activities, the information they gather was not intended to be used to verify compliance with limits in other arms control agreements. Instead, Open Skies is designed as a confidence-building measure that will promote openness and enhance mutual understanding about military activities. The treaty entered into force on January 1, 2002. It currently has 34 participating member states that have conducted more than 835 observation flights since the treaty entered into force.

---

[27] "Chief of the General Staff Makes a Policy Speech," *WPS: What the Papers Say.* WPS Russian Media Monitoring Agency. May 8, 2007; "Russian Move on Key Arms Treaty Not Linked to US ABM Plans," *BBC Monitoring News File.* April 26, 2007.

[28] For details contact Amy F. Woolf, Specialist in National Defense, 7-2379.

Open Skies was originally proposed by President Eisenhower in 1955. In the years before satellites began to collect intelligence data, aerial overflights were seen as a way to gain information needed for both intelligence and confidence-building purposes. The Soviet Union rejected President Eisenhower's proposal because it considered the overflights equal to espionage. President George H. W. Bush revived the Open Skies proposal in May 1989. By this time, both the United States and Soviet Union employed satellites and remote sensors for intelligence collection, so aircraft overflights would add little for that objective. But, at the time when Europe was emerging from the East-West divide of the Cold War, the United States supported increased transparency throughout Europe as a way to reduce the chances of military confrontation and to build confidence among the participants. The Senate consented to the ratification of the treaty on August 6, 1993, and President Clinton signed the instruments of ratification on November 3, 1993, but entry-into-force was delayed until Russia and Belarus approved ratification in May 2001.

The Provisions of Open Skies

The parties to the Open Skies Treaty have agreed to make all of their territory accessible to overflights by unarmed fixed wing observation aircraft. They can restrict flights over areas, such as nuclear power plants, where safety is a concern, but they cannot impede or prohibit flights over any area, including military installations that are considered secret or otherwise off-limits. In most cases, the nation conducting the observation flight will provide the aircraft and sensors for the flight. However, Russia insisted that the Treaty permit the observed country to provide the aircraft if it chose to do so. Nations can also team up to conduct overflights to share the costs of the effort or use aircraft and sensor suites provided by other nations. Each nation is assigned a quota of overflights that it can conduct and must be willing to receive each year. The quota is determined, generally, by the size of the nation's territory. For the United States, this quota is equal to 42 observation flights per year.

The Treaty permits the nations to use several types of sensors—including photographic cameras, infrared cameras, and synthetic aperture radars—during their observation flights. The permitted equipment will allow the nations to collect basic information on military forces and activities, but it will provide them with little detailed technical intelligence. For example, the resolution on the sensors would allow the nations to identify vehicles and distinguish between tanks and trucks, but probably will not allow them to tell one type of tank from another. Each observation flight will produce two sets of data—one for the observing nation and one for the observed nation. Other parties to the Treaty can purchase copies of the data. Each nation is responsible for its own analysis of the data. The participants may have to revisit the agreement's list of permitted sensors in coming years, as technology has moved forward. For example, the permitted cameras use film that is no longer available, and parts that are no longer supported by most manufacturers. But some parties are uncomfortable with the idea of changing to digital imaging, as the images can be enhanced by computers. This would provide more information than is permitted with the current cameras.

The Open Skies Treaty was designed as a confidence-building measure, allowing all nations, including those without access to satellites, to collect information on military forces and activities of other parties to the Treaty. It is not designed to provide detailed intelligence information or data needed to verify compliance with arms control limits. Instead, it allows the participants to gain an improved understanding of military activities in other nations. Overflights may provide early signs of efforts to build up military forces or, conversely, assurances that an adversary or neighbor is not preparing its military for a possible conflict. In any case, it is designed to promote openness and transparency as a way to ease tensions and reduce the likelihood of misunderstandings about military intentions.

Implementation

Although several of the participating nations conducted practice missions in the years before the Treaty entered into force, the first official overflight mission occurred in 2002. The United States has not only conducted several missions over territories in Europe and the former Soviet Union, it has also hosted numerous observation flights over its own territory. It also, occasionally, uses its open skies aircraft to monitor natural disasters, such as the recent earthquake in Haiti. The treaty has proved durable, with flights continuing for several years. They have even proceeded during the early months of 2014, when tensions in the region rose over Russia's interference in Ukraine.

For Further Reading

CRS Report 95-1098 F, *The Open Skies Treaty: Observation Overflights of Military Activities.* (Out of print. For copies contact Amy Woolf, 7-2379.)

The Missile Technology Control Regime

The United States, Canada, France, Germany, Italy, Japan, and the United Kingdom established the Missile Technology Control Regime (MTCR) on April 16, 1987. Designed to slow the proliferation of ballistic and cruise missiles, rockets, and unmanned air vehicles (UAV) capable of delivering weapons of mass destruction, the MTCR is an informal, voluntary arrangement in which participants agree to adhere to common export policy guidelines applied to an "annex" that lists controlled items. Partner-countries adopt the guidelines as national policy and are responsible for restraining their own missile-related transfers. In addition, partners regularly exchange information on relevant export licensing issues, including denials of technology transfers. The MTCR has neither an independent means to verify whether states are adhering to its guidelines or monitor nor a mechanism to penalize states if they violate them.

The MTCR is based on the premise that foreign acquisition or development of delivery systems can be delayed and made more difficult and expensive if major producers restrict exports. Analysts credit the MTCR with slowing missile development in Brazil and India, blocking a cooperative missile program of Argentina, Egypt, and Iraq, and eliminating missile programs in South Africa and Hungary. Moreover, partner countries have tightened their export control laws and procedures, and several have taken legal action against alleged missile-technology smugglers. On the other hand, some analysts note that the MTCR does not regulate countries' acquisition or production of missiles and cannot prevent non-partners from exporting missiles and technology. It has also been difficult to restrain exports of ballistic and cruise missile technology from some Partners—Russia has exported technology to Iran and Great Britain has done so to the United Arab Emirates. In addition, many analysts have argued that advances in missile-related technology will challenge the MTCR's future ability to check missile proliferation. Analysts and experts in the international community have also discussed the possibility that the "supply side" approach of the MTCR has outlived its usefulness and that a "demand side" approach to proliferation, on a regional or global basis, might prove more effective.

Participants

Since 1987, the number of MTCR partners has grown from seven to 34, with Bulgaria joining the Regime in June 2004.[29] Several non-partners, including China, Israel, Romania, Slovakia, and India, have said they will restrict their transfers of missile equipment and technology according to the MTCR.

Membership in the Regime is decided by consensus. According to former MTCR Chairman Per Fischer, "[p]otential members are reviewed on a case-by case basis, and decisions regarding applications are based on the effectiveness of a state's export controls ... its potential contribution to the regime and its proliferation record."[30] The United States supports new requests for membership to the regime only if the country in question agrees not to develop or acquire missiles (excluding space launch vehicles) that exceed MTCR guidelines.

Substance of the MTCR

The MTCR guidelines[31] call on each partner country to exercise restraint when considering transfers of equipment or technology, as well as "intangible" transfers, that would provide, or help a recipient country build, a missile capable of delivering a 500 kilogram (1,100 pound) warhead to a range of 300 kilometers (186 miles) or more. The 500 kilogram weight threshold was intended to limit transfers of missiles that could carry a relatively crude nuclear warhead. A 1993 addition to the guidelines calls for particular restraint in the export of any missiles or related technology if the nation controlling the export judges that the missiles are intended to be used for the delivery of weapons of mass destruction (nuclear, chemical, or biological). Thus some missiles with warheads weighing less than 500 kilograms also fall under MTCR guidelines. From time to time, Regime partners update the MTCR guidelines and annex.

The MTCR annex contains two categories of controlled items. Category I items are the most sensitive. There is "a strong presumption to deny such transfers," according to the MTCR guidelines. Regime partners have greater flexibility in exports of Category II items.

Category I items include complete rocket systems (including ballistic missiles, space launch vehicles, and sounding rockets), UAV systems (including cruise missiles systems, target and reconnaissance drones), production facilities for such systems, and major subsystems (including rocket stages, re-entry vehicles, rocket engines, guidance systems, and warhead mechanisms). Transfers of Category I production facilities are not to be authorized. Category II items are other less sensitive and dual-use missile-related components that could be used to develop a Category I system, and complete missiles and major subsystems of missiles capable of delivering a payload of any size to a range of 300 km.

---

[29] Information on MTCR partners is available at http://www.mtcr.info/english/partners html.

[30] "20 Years of the Missile Technology Control Regime and Beyond," paper given to the DIIS Conference on Missile Proliferation, Copenhagen, May 2, 2007.

[31] The MTCR guidelines and annex are available at http://www mtcr.info.

Hague Code of Conduct Against Ballistic Missile Proliferation (HCOC)

The Hague Code of Conduct Against Ballistic Missile Proliferation (HCOC) was inaugurated on November 25, 2002. As of February 11, 2014, 137 countries subscribed to the Code.[32] The HCOC is not a treaty but instead a set of "fundamental behavioral norms and a framework for cooperation to address missile proliferation." It focuses on the possession of ballistic missiles, as a complement to the supply-side-oriented MTCR. Subscribing states have held regular conferences since the Code came into effect.

The Code intends to "prevent and curb the proliferation of Ballistic Missile systems capable of delivering weapons of mass destruction." It calls on subscribing states "to exercise maximum possible restraint in the development, testing and deployment of Ballistic Missiles capable of delivering weapons of mass destruction [WMD], including, where possible, to reduce national holdings of such missiles." Subscribing states also agree not to assist ballistic missile programs in countries suspected of developing WMD. The HCOC also calls for subscribing states to "exercise the necessary vigilance" in assisting other countries' space-launch programs, which could serve as covers for ballistic missile programs.

Additionally, subscribing states "resolve to implement" several transparency measures, such as producing annual declarations that provide outlines of their ballistic missile policies, as well as "information on the number and generic class" of such missiles launched during the preceding year. The Code also calls on subscribing states to provide similar annual declarations regarding their "expendable Space Launch Vehicle" programs.

Furthermore, the HCOC calls on states to "exchange pre-launch notifications on their Ballistic Missile and Space Launch Vehicle launches and test flights." Signatories are required to provide such notifications to Austria, which serves as the Immediate Central Contact and Executive Secretariat for the HCOC. The United States and Russia each provide such notifications and the annual declarations described above.

The Wassenaar Arrangement[33]

In July 1996, 33 nations approved the Wassenaar Arrangement (formally titled the Wassenaar Arrangement on Export Controls for Conventional Arms and Dual-Use Goods and Technologies) on export controls for conventional arms and dual-use goods and technologies.[34] This agreement replaces the Coordinating Committee For Multilateral Export Controls (CoCom)—the Cold War organization that controlled sensitive exports of technologies to Communist nations.

According to its Guidelines and Procedures, the Wassenaar Arrangement is not formally targeted at "any state or group of states." But it is "intended to enhance co-operation to prevent the acquisition of armaments and sensitive dual-use items for military end-uses, if the situation in a region or the behaviour of a state is, or becomes, a cause for serious concern."[35]

---

[32] The full text is available at http://www.bmeia.gv.at/fileadmin/user_upload/bmeia/media/2-Aussenpolitik_Zentrale/114_hcoc.pdf.

[33] For details, contact Richard Grimmett, Specialist in National Defense, 7-7675.

[34] Dual-use goods are those commodities, processes, or technologies used primarily for civilian purposes which can also be used to develop or enhance the capabilities of military equipment.

[35] The Arrangement's Guidelines and Procedures may be found at http://www.wassenaar.org/guidelines/index html.

The Arrangement, which has 41 members, is designed "to contribute to regional and international security and stability, by promoting transparency and greater responsibility in transfers of conventional arms and dual-use goods and technologies, thus preventing destabilizing accumulations." Member decisions are made by consensus. This group has a broader membership but smaller lists of controlled goods than did CoCom. Its control regime is also less rigorous. Under Wassenaar, each national government regulates its own exports, whereas under CoCom, any member could disapprove any other members' export by of a controlled item to a proscribed destination. There is also no mechanism to punish a Participating State for violating Wassenaar guidelines.

Membership

The Arrangement's guidelines specify that several factors must be considered when deciding on a potential new member's eligibility. These include whether the state has adopted the Arrangement's control lists "as a reference in its national export controls," the government's "adherence to fully effective export controls," and whether the state adheres to several other multilateral agreements.[36]

Items Controlled

Participating States agree to control exports and retransfers of items on a Munitions List and a List of Dual-Use Goods and Technologies. The decision to allow or deny transfer of an item is the sole responsibility of each Participating State. The control lists are updated frequently.

Organization and Operations

Twice a year Participating States report all transfers or licenses issued for sensitive dual-use goods or technology and all deliveries of items on the Munitions List. The data exchange identifies the supplier, recipient, and items transferred.

Participating States also report denials of licenses to transfer items on the Dual-Use list to non-member states. The Arrangement does not prohibit a participating country from making an export that has been denied by another participant (this practice is called "undercutting"). But participants are required to report soon after they approve a license for an export of dual-use goods that are essentially identical to those that have been denied by another participant during the previous three years.

During plenary and working group discussions, Participating States voluntarily share information on potential threats to peace and stability and examine dangerous acquisition trends. The participants review the scope of reporting and coordinating national control policies and develop further guidelines and procedures. Twice a year, the group reviews the Munitions List with a view to extending information and notifications.

---

[36] These agreements include the guidelines for the Nuclear Suppliers Group, the Zangger Committee, the Missile Technology Control Regime, and the Australia Group. They also include the Nuclear Non-Proliferation Treaty, the Biological and Toxicological Weapons Convention, and the Chemical Weapons Convention.

Weapons Control and Elimination Conventions

Chemical Weapons Convention

The Chemical Weapons Convention (CWC) bans the development, production, transfer, stockpiling, and use of chemical and toxin weapons, mandates the destruction of all chemical weapons production facilities, and seeks to control the production and international transfer of the key chemical components of these weapons. Negotiations began in 1968, but made little progress for many years.[37] Verification issues, in particular, stalled the talks until the Soviet Union accepted challenge inspections. In September 1992, the Conference on Disarmament's 40 member-nations agreed on the final draft for the Convention, and it opened for signature in January 1993. As of October 14, 2013, 190 nations had ratified the treaty, which entered into force April 29, 1997. Two states have signed but not ratified the Convention.[38] Five nations have not signed the CWC.[39] Under the Convention, states-parties provide declarations, which detail chemical weapons-related activities or materials and relevant industrial activities, to the Organization for the Prohibition of Chemical Weapons (OPCW). The OPCW inspects and monitors states-parties' facilities and activities that are relevant to the convention.

The U.S. Senate held hearings and debated the CWC for more than four years before consenting to its ratification on April 24, 1997. Congress passed the CWC implementing legislation, as a part of the FY1999 Omnibus Appropriations Act (P.L. 105-277), in late October 1998. This legislation provides the statutory authority for U.S. domestic compliance with the Convention's provisions. The legislation also provides detailed procedures to be used for on-site inspections by the OPCW, including limitations on access and search warrant procedures, should they be required.

Limits and Restrictions

Parties to the Convention have agreed to cease all offensive chemical weapons research and production and close all relevant facilities. They agreed to declare all chemical weapons stockpiles, allow an inventory by international inspectors, and seal their stocks. They must also destroy their weapons within 10 years, unless the OPCW approves an extension. They must also destroy all chemical weapons production facilities within 10 years. In "exceptional cases of compelling need," the OPCW may approve the conversion of these facilities to peaceful purposes.

The CWC contains a complex verification regime, with different obligations applying to different types of chemical facilities. The Convention establishes three schedules of chemicals, grouped by relevance to chemical weapons production and extent of legitimate peaceful uses. Some facilities are subject to systematic on-site verification, others are subject to periodic verification inspections. Facilities for a third class of chemicals are subject to random or "ad hoc" inspections. Signatories may also request challenge inspections at facilities suspected to be in violation of the Convention. The OPCW will carry out these inspections on short notice. Inspected nations will

---

[37] The United States and Soviet Union—possessors of the world's largest chemical weapons stockpiles—also conducted bilateral negotiations from 1976 to 1980.

[38] Israel, Myanmar.

[39] Angola, Egypt, North Korea, South Sudan.

have the right to negotiate the extent of inspectors' access to any facility, but must make every reasonable effort to confirm compliance.[40]

Destruction Deadlines

According to the OPCW, all of the member-states' declared chemical weapons production facilities have been inactivated and, as of December 2, 2013, almost 82% of declared chemical weapons agent stockpiles had been destroyed.[41] This amount does not include the chemical stockpiles declared by Syria (see below).

Six countries declared possession of chemical weapons, but none destroyed their stocks by the original April 29, 2007, deadline. In July 2007, Albania became the first country to have destroyed its declared chemical weapons. South Korea became the second on July 10, 2008. India became the third on March 16, 2009. Three other states—Libya, Russia, Syria, and the United States—have declared possession of such weapons.

Libya

Libya joined the CWC in January 2004. At that time, Libya declared nearly 25 metric tonnes of bulk sulfur mustard agent, several thousand unloaded aerial munitions designed for use with chemical warfare agents, and several chemical weapons production facilities. The declared aerial munitions were destroyed in March 2004. Production facilities were destroyed or converted under OPCW supervision.

Libya had said that it would destroy its Category One weapons[42] by December 31, 2010, and its Category Two weapons by December 31, 2011.[43] However, Tripoli was given until May 15, 2011, to destroy all of its Category One weapons. As of October 31, 2010, Libya had destroyed approximately 4% of its Category One weapons and over 39% of its Category Two weapons.[44] These weapons, which included some undeclared stocks of mustard gas, remained on Libyan territory after the 2011 revolution and fall of the Muammar al Qadhafi regime. Libya's Permanent Representative to the OPCW stated March 11, 2011, that the country's "situation regarding the chemical weapons to be destroyed remains unchanged and under control."[45] In January 2012, OPCW inspectors returned to Libya to verify the status of Libya's chemical weapons stockpiles. In 2013, Libya completed the destruction of its stock of bulk mustard agent. Libya announced in January 2014 that it had completed destruction of the CW filled munitions it had discovered and

---

[40] For more information on CWC verification issues, see CRS Report RL31559, *Proliferation Control Regimes: Background and Status*, coordinated by Mary Beth D. Nikitin.

[41] Opening Statement by the Director-General to the Conference of the States Parties at its Eighteenth Session, C-18/DG.17, December 2, 2013.

[42] Chemical weapons are grouped into three categories, depending on the weapon type.

[43] Organization for the Prohibition of Chemical Weapons, Status Report On The Progress Made By Those States Parties That Have Been Granted Extensions Of Deadlines For The Destruction Of Their Category 1 Chemical Weapons, November 14, 2008.

[44] Organization for the Prohibition of Chemical Weapons, "Opening Statement by the Director-General to the Conference of the States," C-15/DG.14, November 29, 2010.

[45] http://www.opcw.org/news/article/opcw-director-general-meets-permanent-representative-of-the-libyan-arab-jamahiriya/.

declared in 2011 and 2012.[46] The U.S. Department of Defense Cooperative Threat Reduction (CTR) program provided $52 million toward this effort, in collaboration with Germany. Its stocks of Category 2 (precursor) chemicals are to be destroyed by 2016.

Syria[47]

The Obama Administration threatened military action against Syria in response to chemical weapons use in Syria in August 2013. In a diplomatic solution that resulted in the Administration withdrawing the threat, Syria agreed to join the international Chemical Weapons Convention (CWC), which requires Syria to destroy all of its chemical weapons stocks and production facilities.[48] Based on a joint U.S.-Russian proposal, the Executive Council of the Organization for the Prohibition of Chemical Weapons (OPCW) approved a destruction plan under which Syria is required to destroy all chemical weapons by June 30, 2014. Under Security Council Resolution 2118, the OPCW is to report to the U.N. Security Council on implementation on a monthly basis.

A joint mission of U.N. and OPCW personnel was created to monitor and facilitate Syrian chemical weapons disarmament.[49] OPCW-U.N. experts arrived in Damascus on October 1, 2013, and began to inspect Syria's declared chemical weapons facilities. The OPCW spokesman told reporters on October 31 that the Syrian government met the November 1, 2013, destruction deadline for disabling production equipment, and that all chemical weapons stocks and agents in Syria were under "tamper-proof" seal. The first stage of destruction activities focused on destroying "critical equipment" at chemical weapons production facilities and mixing and filling units.

The current stage of the chemical weapons destruction process involves transportation and removal of chemical weapons agents from the country. These are liquid chemicals that have not been loaded into delivery vehicles. The OPCW Executive Council on November 14, 2013, approved the destruction of Syria's chemical weapons agents ("priority 1" chemicals) outside of Syria due to the security situation in the country. The United States and others have provided equipment to the OPCW-U.N. Joint Mission to help safely transfer these chemicals from storage facilities to the Syrian port of Latakia. Once all the chemicals are at the port, Danish and Norwegian ships are to pick up the chemicals and remove them from Syria. The first quantity of priority chemicals was moved to the port of Latakia in early January 2014.

No country had agreed to conduct destruction operations on its territory due to public concerns about the dangers of the material, but also due to the short timeline for destruction, which in some cases would not have allowed for the required environmental and health impact assessments. Therefore, the United States plans to neutralize the liquid chemical weapons agents on board the Maritime Administration's Motor Vessel (MV) Cape Ray using newly installed field deployable hydrolysis systems (FDHS). This ship is expected to receive 700 metric tons of both mustard

---

[46] https://www.opcw.org/news/article/libya-completes-destruction-of-its-category-1-chemical-weapons/.

[47] For more information on chemical weapons in Syria, see CRS Report R42848, *Syria's Chemical Weapons: Issues for Congress*, coordinated by Mary Beth D. Nikitin.

[48] Syria is believed to have more than 1,000 metric tons of chemical warfare agents and precursor chemicals. This stockpile includes several hundred metric tons of the nerve agent sarin, which represents the bulk of Syria's chemical weapons stockpile. Damascus also has several hundred metric tons of mustard agent in ready-to-use form and several metric tons of the nerve agent VX.

[49] See http://opcw.unmissions.org/.

agent and DF compound, a key component in sarin.[50] U.S. personnel, including 64 Army chemical specialists, will run the operation. The MV Cape Ray is now at the port of Rota, Spain. Once removed from Latakia, the most dangerous compounds in approximately 60 containers will be transferred to the Cape Ray at the Italian port of Gioia Tauro for destruction at sea in international waters. NATO has canceled cooperation with the Russian Federation on guarding the Cape Ray during chemical weapons destruction activities because of Russia's actions in Ukraine.[51] Less sensitive chemicals will be shipped to commercial processing facilities, for example in the United Kingdom. Companies in Finland and the United States were awarded contracts for processing the liquid waste (effluent) from the destruction process.[52]

Syria did not meet the original deadline of December 31, 2013, for removal of these agents from its territory. According to the OPCW Director General, the delays were caused by "security concerns, the procurement and delivery of large quantities of packaging and transportation materials and equipment, and adverse weather conditions."[53] Reports in early January quoted a Syrian government official as saying two CW storage sites have been under attack.[54] The Syrian government also missed a February 5, 2014, deadline, raising questions about the intentions of the Syrian government. Syria has asked for a new deadline of mid-May. In February, the UN Security Council called upon Syria to expedite removal of the chemicals.

In March 2014, OPCW-UN Joint Mission Special Coordinator Sigrid Kaag described "important progress" in efforts to expedite the transfer and destruction of chemicals and encouraged the Syrian government "to sustain the current pace."[55] As of April 8, Secretary Kerry confirmed the March 20 Joint Mission estimate that the Syrian government had moved 11 shipments of chemicals to the port of Latakia, representing around 53.6% of total stocks to be removed.[56]

The Syrian government also did not meet the deadline of March 15, 2014, for destruction of its 12 chemical weapons production facilities, and has proposed that the facilities not be completely destroyed but instead made inaccessible.[57] The CWC requires that production facilities be "physically destroyed." U.S. Ambassador to the OPCW Robert Mikulak said in a February statement that the Executive Council should require Syria to physically destroy the facilities in line with the Convention.[58] The OPCW is now working on a destruction plan for these facilities with Syria.

---

[50] "Army to Destroy Syrian Chemical Weapons Aboard Ship," *Army News Service*, January 3, 2014.

[51] "NATO to cancel activities with Russia, step up military cooperation with Ukraine," *Stars and Stripes*, March 6, 2014.

[52] "OPCW awards contracts to two companies for destruction of Syrian chemical and effluents," OPCW-UN Joint Mission Press Release February 14, 2014, http://opcw.unmissions.org/AboutOPCWUNJointMission/tabid/54/ctl/Details/mid/651/ItemID/182/Default.aspx.

[53] "Director General says Removal of Priority Chemicals in Syria Marks Important New Phase in Work of Joint Mission," OPCW press release, January 8, 2014.

[54] Nick Cumming-Bruce and Rick Gladstone, "Syrian Government Reports 2 Attacks on Chemical Arms Sites," *New York Times*, January 8, 2014.

[55] "Over half of Syria's chemical weapons removed or destroyed, says joint OPCW-UN mission," UN News Centre, March 20, 2014.

[56] Ibid.; and Secretary of State John Kerry Testimony before the Senate Foreign Relations Committee, April 8, 2014.

[57] "Syria to miss deadline to destroy 12 chemical arms sites," *Reuters*, March 6, 2014.

[58] http://www.state.gov/t/avc/rls/2014/221891.htm.

Despite these delays, however, UN officials say they are optimistic that the final deadline, June 30, 2014, for destruction of all chemical weapons and production facilities will be met.

Russia

As of October 31, 2013, Russia had destroyed more than 77% of its Category One chemical weapons stocks; Moscow has destroyed its Category Two and Category Three chemical weapons stockpiles.[59] The CWC Conference of States-Parties gave Russia until December 31, 2009, to destroy 45% of its Category One stockpiles and until April 29, 2012, to destroy the rest.[60] Russia did not meet the 2012 deadline, but plans to destroy its stockpiles by December 2015.[61]

Under DOD's Cooperative Threat Reduction Program, the United States has provided Russia with considerable financial assistance for chemical weapons destruction.[62] The impetus for continued funding, despite reservations about this program, has been the concern that the Russian chemical weapons stockpile is a potential source of chemical weapons proliferation.

The United States

The United States has also encountered difficulties in destroying its Category One chemical weapons stockpile and did not meet its deadline for doing so. Washington has already destroyed all of its Category Three stockpile and has declared no Category Two weapons. In April 2006, the United States submitted its formal request to the OPCW Chairman and Director-General to extend the United States' final chemical weapons destruction deadline from April 2007 to April 29, 2012, the latest possible date allowed under the CWC.[63] However, Ambassador Eric Javits, then-U.S. Permanent Representative to the OPCW, added that "we do not expect to be able to meet that deadline" because Washington had encountered "delays and difficulties" in destroying its stockpile.[64] These delays have generally resulted from the need to meet state and federal environmental requirements and from both local and congressional concerns over the means of destruction.

The 2008 Defense Appropriations Act (P.L. 110-116) required the Defense Department to "complete work on the destruction" of the U.S. chemical weapons stockpile by the 2012 deadline "and in no circumstances later than December 31, 2017." Additionally, the National Defense Authorization Act for Fiscal Year 2008 (P.L. 110-181) required that the Secretary of Defense submit a report to Congress that included a

> description of the options and alternatives for accelerating the completion of chemical weapons destruction at each such facility, particularly in time to meet the [CWC] destruction deadline of April 29, 2012 ... and by December 31, 2017.

---

[59] C-18/DG.17, December 2, 2013.

[60] "Opening Statement by the Director-General to the Conference of the States," C-15/DG.14, November 29, 2010.

[61] C-18/DG.17, December 2, 2013.

[62] CRS Report R43143, *The Evolution of Cooperative Threat Reduction: Issues for Congress*, by Mary Beth D. Nikitin and Amy F. Woolf.

[63] Ambassador Eric Javits, U.S. Permanent Representative to the OPCW, Statement Concerning Request to Extend the United States' Destruction Deadline Under the Chemical Weapons Convention, April 20, 2006. http://www.state.gov/t/isn/rls/rm/64878 htm.

[64] Ibid.

That report, submitted in June 2008, compared three options for accelerating stockpile destruction, noting that "[t]here are no options to achieve 100 percent destruction of the national stockpile by 2012."[65] The three options were:

- Provide schedule incentives authorized by Congress[66] to ensure that the operating sites complete the destruction of their stockpiles by 2012.

- Transport portions of the remaining stockpile to destruction facilities which are already operating.

- Accelerate the destruction schedule for the Colorado and Kentucky sites.

According to a 2013 Department of Defense report, the "currently planned destruction operations" are not "expected to accommodate the December 31, 2017, congressionally-mandated destruction deadline." The report adds that the department "continues to evaluate options to improve the destruction schedule without sacrificing worker and public safety and security."[67]

As of December 2, 2013, the United States had destroyed almost 90% of its Category One stockpile.[68] Washington projects that its two destruction facilities under construction will destroy the remaining chemical agents stockpiles located at Pueblo, CO, and Lexington, KY. According to the 2013 Defense Department report, these stockpiles are to be destroyed by November 2019 and September 2023, respectively.[69]

Iraq

Iraq used chemical weapons during its 1980-1988 war with Iran and against Iraqi Kurds in 1988. Following the 1991 Persian Gulf War, the UN Security Council adopted Resolution 687 on April 3, 1991. This resolution was the first in a series of resolutions that required Iraq to declare its programs for nuclear, chemical, and biological weapons, as well as missiles with ranges exceeding 150 kilometers, and to destroy the weapons and related materials under UN monitoring. Regarding chemical weapons, Resolution 687 required Iraq to "unconditionally accept the destruction, removal, or rendering harmless, under international supervision of ... [a]ll chemical and biological weapons and all stocks of agents and all related subsystems and components and all research, development, support and manufacturing facilities." The resolutions also required Baghdad to accept an ongoing UN monitoring regime to prevent Iraqi reconstitution of its prohibited weapons programs. The UN Secretary-General subsequently formed the United Nations Special Commission (UNSCOM) to verify Iraq's compliance with the resolution.

Iraq's chemical weapons generally met one of four fates: they were used during the Iran-Iraq war;[70] they were destroyed by Iraq under UNSCOM supervision; they were secretly destroyed by Iraq outside UNSCOM supervision; or they were destroyed by coalition forces during the 1991

---

[65] Department of Defense Report, *Chemical Demilitarization Program Semi-Annual Report to Congress,* 2008.

[66] In §923 of P.L. 109-364.

[67] Department of Defense Report, *Chemical Demilitarization Program Semi-Annual Report to Congress,* September 2013.

[68] C-18/DG.17, December 2, 2013. The United States has destroyed all of its chemical weapons munitions.

[69] Ibid.

[70] Iraq used more than 75% of its chemical weapons during the Iran-Iraq war, according to figures from Saddam Hussein's government.

Persian Gulf War. Although "a number of issues relating to Iraq's chemical weapons programme remain unresolved," according to a 2006 UN report,[71] the inspectors "were able to identify the major parameters of this programme, its scope and the results achieved." Moreover, the "vast majority" of chemical agents and munitions which Iraq possessed in 1991 were "declared by Iraq, identified by the inspectors and destroyed under international supervision," according to the report.[72]

Iraq's legacy chemical weapons are "contained in two sealed bunkers" at an old Iraqi chemical weapons production facility, according to a July 31, 2012, British Ministry of Defense statement.[73] These weapons were "left over after being rendered unusable by the UN inspection teams," OPCW Director-General Ambassador Ahmet Üzümcü said in a June 6, 2013 speech. Iraq acceded to the CWC in 2009 and is working with the OCPW and countries such Germany, Switzerland, and the United Kingdom to devise an appropriate disposal method for these weapons. Iraq "has recently submitted to the Secretariat the detailed facility information for the destruction of its chemical weapons," the Director-General said in December 2013.[74]

On June 11, 2014, the Islamic State of Iraq and the Levant invaded the al-Muthanna chemical weapons facility. Due to this situation, Permanent Representative of Iraq, Mohamed Alhakim, stated in a June 30, 2014 letter to UN Secretary–General Ban Ki-moon that Iraq is currently "unable to fulfil its obligations to destroy chemical weapons" and will resume these "obligations as soon as the security situation has improved and control of the facility has been regained."[75]

Other Compliance Issues

A State Department report covering 2012 raised some compliance questions, but did not conclude that any CWC state-party had a chemical weapons program in violation of the Convention.[76]

Biological Weapons Convention

In 1969, the Nixon Administration unilaterally renounced U.S. biological weapons. Offensive BW development and production ceased, and destruction of the U.S. BW stockpile began. Simultaneously, the United States pressed the Soviet Union to follow its example. After some delay, agreement was reached, and the Biological Weapons Convention (BWC)[77] was signed in 1972. The United States, after lengthy Senate consultations, ratified the Convention in 1975, the same year that the Convention entered into force.

---

[71] *Summary of the Compendium of Iraq's Proscribed Weapons Programmes*, June 2006.

[72] UNSCOM personnel left Iraq in late 1998, but returned in late 2002 and worked in the country until just before the U.S.-led invasion of Iraq in March 2003. Neither the inspectors nor coalition troops found any significant evidence of renewed prohibited Iraqi weapons programs.

[73] "MOD Experts to Help Iraqis Destroy Legacy Chemical Weapons," July 31, 2012.

[74] C-18/DG.17, December 2, 2013.

[75] http://www.un.org/ga/search/view_doc.asp?symbol=S/2014/457.

[76] *Compliance with the Convention on the Prohibition of the Development, Production, Stockpiling and Use of Chemical Weapons and on Their Destruction*, Condition (10)(C) Report, Department of State, January 2013.

[77] The agreement if more formally known as the Convention on the Prohibition of the Development, Production and Stockpiling of Bacteriological (Biological) and Toxin Weapons and on Their Destruction. The text of the BWC and associated documents are available at http://www.un.org/disarmament/WMD/Bio/index.shtml.

The BWC bans the development, production, stockpiling, and transfer of biological weapons, as well as biological agents and toxins. It also bans "equipment or means of delivery designed to use such agents or toxins for hostile purposes or in armed conflict." In addition, the Convention requires States-Parties to destroy all relevant "agents, toxins, weapons, equipment and means of delivery."

The BWC permits only defensive biological warfare research (e.g., vaccines, protective equipment) and allows production and stockpiling of BW agents only in amounts justifiable for protective or peaceful purposes. Unlike the Chemical Weapons Convention (CWC), the BWC does not specify particular biological agents, but generically defines them as "microbial or other biological agents or toxins whatever their origin or method of production, of types and in quantities that have no justification for prophylactic or peaceful purposes."

As of April 22, 2014, the Convention had 170 States Parties, including the United States, and there were 10 additional countries that have signed, but not ratified the Convention. The Convention does not contain any independent verification or enforcement mechanisms.[78]

Verification and Enforcement

The Fifth Review Conference of the BWC, which took place in November 2001, ended in disarray, with the parties unable to agree upon a final declaration. The primary deadlock was the issue of an adaptive protocol to the Convention, intended to enhance its enforcement. In July 2001, after almost seven years of negotiations, the United States declared the 200-page protocol unacceptable as basis for further negotiation. A Bush Administration review concluded that the draft protocol would not provide adequate security against covert violations, yet could endanger the security of U.S. biodefense programs and U.S. commercial proprietary information. Alone in its complete rejection of the draft protocol, the United States came under widespread international criticism, including from close allies, for "jeopardizing" the future of biological arms control. In response, the Administration put forward several proposals at the 2001 Review Conference, urging their adoption by BWC State Parties at the national level. These included

- Criminalization of BWC violations and expedited extradition procedures for violators.

- United Nations investigation of suspicious disease outbreaks or alleged BW use.

- Procedures for addressing BWC compliance concerns.

- Improved international disease control.

- Improved security over research on pathogenic organisms.

The Review Conference was unable to reach a compromise final declaration on future activities satisfactory to all State Parties, and adjourned until November 2002. The United States has continued to oppose further negotiations on verification. Confronted with the U.S. position, the chairman of the 2002 Review Conference presented a minimal program emphasizing only annual

---

[78] Article V of the Convention does speak to the issue of compliance, stating that the States Parties "undertake to consult one another and to cooperate in solving any problems which may arise in relation to the objective of, or in the application of the provisions of, the Convention. Consultation and Cooperation pursuant to this article may also be undertaken through appropriate international procedures within the framework of the United Nations and in accordance with its Charter."

meetings to discuss strengthening national laws and ways to respond to BW attacks. These were endorsed by the United States and accepted by the conference.

The 6th BWC Review Conference, held in December 2006, could not reach consensus on a comprehensive set of guidelines for national implementation of the Convention owing to differences between the United States and the non-aligned nations group over technology transfer control issues. The assumption of U.S. opposition also precluded consideration of enhanced verification or enforcement provisions for the Convention. The conference, however, did establish a new program of work for annual meetings, which took place before the 7th Review Conference in December 2011. The meetings included discussion and information exchanges on a variety of issues, including domestic enforcement of BWC provisions, pathogen security, and oversight of potentially dual-use research. The United States required, however, that these sessions be prohibited from reaching binding decisions. Beginning in 2007, the BWC States-Parties have met annually.

The Obama Administration has chosen not to support revival of the negotiations on a BWC verification protocol, Under Secretary for Arms Control and International Security Ellen Tauscher announced in a December 9, 2009, address to the BWC states-parties. The Administration has "determined that a legally binding protocol would not achieve meaningful verification or greater security," she explained, adding

> [t]he ease with which a biological weapons program could be disguised within legitimate activities and the rapid advances in biological research make it very difficult to detect violations. We believe that a protocol would not be able to keep pace with the rapidly changing nature of the biological weapons threat.

Instead, Tauscher stated, the United States believes that "confidence in BWC compliance should be promoted by enhanced transparency about activities and pursuing compliance diplomacy to address concerns." Pointing out that part of the November 2009 U.S. National Strategy for Countering Biological Threats[79] is to "reinvigorate" the BWC, Tauscher exhorted the Convention's states-parties to join the United States in "increasing transparency, improving confidence building measures and engaging in more robust bilateral compliance discussions." She proposed such measures as increasing participation in the Convention's Confidence-Building Measures,[80] as well as bilateral and multilateral cooperation in such areas as pathogen security and disease surveillance and response. Secretary of State Hillary Clinton reiterated U.S. opposition to a BWC "verification regime" in a December 7, 2011, address to the BWC Review Conference.

The United States identified several goals for the 2011 Review Conference, including

- promoting universality of the BWC;

- enhancing confidence in states-parties' compliance with the Convention via transparency measures and "mechanisms for consultation and clarification";

- pursuing a "strengthened, revitalized intersessional process";

---

[79] http://www.whitehouse.gov/sites/default/files/National_Strategy_for_Countering_BioThreats.pdf.

[80] These measures are vehicles for BWC states-parties to share information about their biological activities.

- increasing states' capacity for "disease surveillance and response," including natural disease outbreaks; and

- enhancing efforts to strengthen national implementation and measures to counter the threat of bioterrorism."[81]

The 7th Review Conference was held from December 5-22, 2011. The conference participants decided to continue the intersessional process with some changes. The annual meetings will address three standing agenda items: cooperation and assistance, review of relevant scientific and technological developments, and strengthening national implementation. In addition, during the intersessional program, the states-parties are to discuss enabling fuller participation in BWC-related Confidence Building Measures and strengthening implementation of Article VII of the Convention.[82] The conference did not make any decisions on verification.

Compliance Concerns

No nation publically acknowledges either an offensive biological weapons (BW) program or stockpile. A State Department report covering 2012 does not state that any BWC state-party violated the Convention during that time.[83]

The Arms Trade Treaty

The Arms Trade Treaty (ATT) is a multilateral treaty of unlimited duration. Its stated objectives are to "[e]stablish the highest possible common international standards for regulating or improving the regulation of the international trade in conventional arms ..." and to "[p]revent and eradicate the illicit trade in conventional arms and prevent their diversion."

Though various concepts similar to the ATT have been discussed in international circles for decades, a speech by the UK Foreign Secretary backing the concept in 2004 is widely credited as giving critical momentum to the movement by adding a major conventional arms exporter to it. Beginning in 2006, the treaty was negotiated in the UN General Assembly (UNGA) and specialized fora. A UNGA vote in early April 2013 approved the treaty in its negotiated form, with only Iran, North Korea, and Syria voting against it. Notable abstentions included Russia, a major arms exporter, and emerging powers China and India, the latter being one of the world's largest arms importers. As of April 17, 2014, China, Russia, and India had not signed the treaty.

The ATT opened for signature on June 3, 2013, and will enter into force after 50 signatories deliver their documents of ratification, acceptance, or approval to the UN Secretary-General, who is the Depository. As of April 17, 2014, the treaty had been signed by 118 states, 31 of which had ratified the treaty. The United States participated in the drafting of the ATT and voted for it in the UNGA on April 2, 2013. The United States signed the ATT on September 25, 2013, but has not

---

[81] Statement by Ambassador Laura Kennedy, December 6, 2010; statement by Ambassador Laura Kennedy, January 20, 2011.

[82] Article VII states, "Each State Party to this Convention undertakes to provide or support assistance, in accordance with the United Nations Charter, to any Party to the Convention which so requests, if the Security Council decides that such Party has been exposed to danger as a result of violation of the Convention."

[83] *Adherence to and Compliance With Arms Control, Nonproliferation, and Disarmament Agreements and Commitments*, U.S. Department of State, July 12, 2013.

ratified it. Because the United States already has strong export control laws in place, the ATT would likely require no significant changes to policy, regulations, or law.

The ATT regulates trade in conventional weapons between and among countries. It does not affect sales or trade in weapons among private citizens within a nation. The treaty obligates States Parties engaged in the international arms trade to establish national control systems to review, authorize, and document the import, export, brokerage, transit, and transshipment of conventional weapons, their parts, and ammunition. The treaty also requires that States Parties report on their treaty-specified transfers to other nations on an annual basis to the Secretariat. The scope of the weapons covered by the treaty includes the following, though States Parties may voluntarily include other conventional weapons as well:

- battle tanks,
- armored combat vehicles,
- large-caliber artillery systems,
- combat aircraft,
- attack helicopters,
- warships,
- missiles and missile launchers, and
- small arms and light weapon.

The ATT also binds States Parties to certain pre-export review processes that take into account various criteria related to possible destabilizing effects on international security, terrorism, transnational crime, human rights, and other factors in determining whether or not a transfer should be approved. A State Party is specifically prohibited from approving a transfer to another nation that violates a United Nations Security Council Resolution adopted under Chapter VII of the United Nations Charter, especially an arms embargo. Also explicitly prohibited is any transfer where a State Party "has knowledge" when reviewing the proposed transfer that the treaty-specified arms, parts, or ammunition would be used in the "commission of genocide, crimes against humanity, grave breaches of the Geneva Conventions of 1949, attacks directed against civilian objects or civilians protected as such, or other war crimes as defined by international agreements to which it is a party." Parties to the treaty are obligated to take measures to prevent the illegal diversion of covered arms and ammunition, to mitigate risks of diversion occurring by cooperating with each other and exchanging information, and to "take appropriate measures" if a diversion is detected. States Parties are also encouraged to exchange relevant information about effectively addressing illicit diversion. Finally, the ATT encourages cooperation between States Parties in the development of implementing legislation, institutional capacity building, and other pertinent areas.

After entry into force, the treaty's governing body, the Conference of States Parties, will meet within a year and then thereafter to review the implementation of the treaty with as of yet undetermined frequency. The treaty envisages a minimal Secretariat, whose cost shall be borne by the ATT's States Parties, with a role largely confined to disseminating treaty-related reporting and lists of national points of contact, facilitating and matching offers of assistance, and organizing Conferences of States Parties.

Controlling the Use of Anti-Personnel Landmines

Anti-personnel landmines (APL) are small, inexpensive weapons that kill or maim people upon contact. Abandoned, unmarked minefields can remain dangerous to both soldiers and civilians for an indefinite time. Mines were addressed in *The Convention on Prohibitions or Restrictions on the Use of Certain Conventional Weapons Which May Be Deemed To Be Excessively Injurious or To Have Indiscriminate Effects* also known as the Convention on Conventional Weapons (CCW).[84] Protocol II of this contains rules for marking, registering, and removing minefields. The CCW was concluded in 1980 and entered into force in 1993. The United States signed it in 1982 and the U.S. Senate gave its advice and consent to ratification on March 24, 1995.

U.S. Initiatives

In 1992, Congress established a one year moratorium on U.S. exports of APL (P.L. 102-484) and subsequently extended it for 15 more years (see P.L. 107-115). H.R. 948, introduced in the First Session, 107th Congress, sought to make the ban permanent but was not brought to a vote. Many nations have followed the U.S. example and imposed their own moratoria. In the FY1996 Foreign Operations Appropriations Act (P.L. 104-107) Congress established a one-year ban on the use of APL by U.S. personnel to begin in 1999—but, the 105th Congress repealed the moratorium in the FY1999 Defense Authorization Act (P.L. 105-261).

In 1996, President Clinton announced a policy that immediately discontinued U.S. use of "dumb" APL (except in the DMZ of Korea); supported negotiation of a worldwide ban on APL in the United Nations; and supported development of alternative technologies to perform landmine functions without endangering civilians and expanded mine detection and clearing technology efforts and assistance to mine-plagued countries. This initiative temporarily retained the possible use of "smart" mines that render themselves harmless after a certain period of time, either through self-destruction, self-neutralization, or self-deactivation. Clinton subsequently set a goal of 2003 to replace even smart mines everywhere except Korea, and of 2006 in Korea.

In November 1996, the United States introduced a resolution to the U.N. General Assembly to pursue an international agreement that would ban use, stockpiling, production, and transfer of APL—there were 84 co-sponsors. Some countries, such as Canada, already abided by the intent of the proposed agreement and pushed for an early deadline to reach agreement. Others, however, were concerned that verifying such an agreement would be difficult, or that AP landmines still have a useful and legitimate role in their security planning. Landmine control, specifically a ban on exports, was briefly on the agenda of the Conference on Disarmament (CD) in Geneva for 1999. During 2000, however, that body could not agree on its program of work and the landmine issue was not addressed again.

During 1997, the government of Canada and a number of nongovernmental organizations, such as the International Campaign to Ban Landmines, sponsored conferences to craft a treaty outside the CD process. Over 100 nations signed the Ottawa Treaty, formally titled the *Convention on the Prohibition of the Use, Stockpiling, Production and Transfer of Anti-personnel Mines and on Their Destruction,* which entered into force for its parties on March 1, 1999. As of March 21, 2011, 156 states were party to the treaty. The Clinton Administration participated in the Ottawa Process, but declined to sign the Treaty after failing to gain certain temporary exceptions to treaty

---

[84] *Convention on Certain Conventional Weapons*, http://www.ccwtreaty.com/ccwtreatytext htm.

language. Specifically, the United States wanted to continue to use APL in the defense of South Korea until 2006 if necessary, and the ability to include smart APL (or "devices") within anti-tank landmine munitions. President Clinton suggested that the United States would sign the Ottawa Treaty in 2006 if effective alternatives to APL were available.

The Ottawa Convention requires States-Parties to stop the production, use, and transfer of APL, as well as destroy all stockpiled APL, except for the "minimum number absolutely necessary" for training purposes, within four years. As of April 17, 2014, 133 countries had signed the treaty and 161 countries are states-parties. Six states-parties had not yet destroyed their APL as of December 16, 2013.[85] Belarus, Greece, Turkey, and Ukraine all missed their stockpile destruction deadlines. Turkey completed destroying its APL in June 2011.[86] As of December 16, 2013, the other three governments had not provided specific dates for destroying their stockpiles.[87] Finland, Guinea-Bissau, and Poland must also destroy APL stockpiles. States-Parties are also required to clear APL within 10 years, but can request extensions of up to 10 years to complete this task.[88] Thirty-two states-parties have not yet met their clearance obligations.[89]

The Convention does not include a verification body, but States-Parties may submit allegations of noncompliance, as well as requests for "clarification" from relevant governments, to the U.N. Secretary-General. A State-Party may also request that a special meeting of other treaty members address the compliance matters. States-Parties can initiate fact-finding missions and also request relevant governments to address compliance issues.

In February 2004, the Bush Administration announced that, after 2010, the United States would not use any type of persistent landmines, whether anti-personnel or—a new policy—anti-vehicle. Self-destruct and self-deactivating landmines will be used and will meet or exceed specifications of the Amended Mines Protocol, CCW. It also indicated that alternatives to persistent landmines would be developed that incorporate enhanced technologies. This policy did not include a date to join the Ottawa Treaty. Richard Kidd, Director of the State Department's Office of Weapons Removal and Abatement, said in a November 21, 2007, speech that the United States would not sign the Ottawa Convention. If needed, U.S. forces will use non-persistent mines. Various U.S. landmine systems were reportedly prepositioned in the Middle East in preparation for the 2003 war in Iraq, but were not used.

The Obama Administration is conducting "an on-going comprehensive review of U.S. landmine policy," according to a December 1, 2009, statement. Steven Costner, Deputy Director of the State Department's Office of Weapons Removal and Abatement, stated on December 6, 2012, that the review has "identified operational issues related to accession [to the convention] that require careful consideration. This consideration is ongoing." On June 27, 2014, during the Third Review Conference of the Ottawa Convention, the United States announced that it "will not produce or

---

[85] Meeting of the States Parties to the Convention on the Prohibition of the Use, Stockpiling, Production and Transfer of Anti-Personnel Mines and on Their Destruction, *Final Report Part Two, Achieving the Aims of the Cartagena Action Plan: The Geneva Progress Report 2012-2013*, December 16, 2013. APLC/MSP.13/2013/6/Add.1.

[86] Meeting of the States Parties to the Convention on the Prohibition of the Use, Stockpiling, Production and Transfer of Anti-Personnel Mines and on Their Destruction, *Final Report*, February 16, 2012. APLC/MSP.11/2011/8.

[87] APLC/MSP.13/2013/6/Add.1.

[88] The full text of the Convention may be found at http://www.icbl.org/content/download/7050/165094/file/treatyenglish.pdf.

[89] APLC/MSP.10/2010/WP.8.

otherwise acquire any anti-personnel landmines in the future," including for the purpose of replacing expiring stockpiles. Moreover, the United States is "conducting a high fidelity modeling and simulation effort to ascertain how to mitigate the risks associated with the loss" of such mines.[90] Edward C. Price, a spokesman for the White House National Security Council, affirmed that the United States is "pressing forward to conclusion of an extensive and ongoing review of our land mine policy."[91]

Cluster Munitions[92]

Cluster munitions are weapons that open in mid-air and dispense smaller submunitions—anywhere from a few dozen to hundreds—into an area. They can be delivered by aircraft or from ground systems such as artillery, rockets, and missiles. Cluster munitions are valued militarily because one munition can kill or destroy many targets within its impact area, and fewer weapons systems are needed to deliver fewer munitions to attack multiple targets. They also permit a smaller force to engage a larger adversary and are considered by some an "economy of force" weapon. On the other hand, critics note that cluster munitions disperse their large numbers of submunitions imprecisely over an extended area, that they frequently fail to detonate and are difficult to detect, and that the submunitions can remain explosive hazards for decades. They can also produce high civilian casualties if they are fired into areas where soldiers and civilians are intermixed or if inaccurate cluster munitions land in populated areas.

There are two major ongoing international initiatives to regulate cluster munitions:

U.N. Convention on Prohibitions or Restrictions on the Use of Certain Conventional Weapons (CCW)

In an effort to restrict or ban specific types of weapons used in armed conflicts, 51 states negotiated the CCW in 1980.[93] When the treaty entered into force in December 1983, it applied only to incendiary weapons, mines and booby-traps, and weapons intended to cause casualties through very small fragments. Since then, some states parties have added provisions through additional protocols to address other types of weapons. Negotiations on cluster munitions are carried out under Protocol V on Explosive Remnants of War. Acting in accordance with the recommendation of a group of experts established during the 2006 CCW review conference, states-parties to the convention decided in 2007 to "negotiate a proposal to address urgently the humanitarian impact of cluster munitions."[94] The experts group continued negotiations in 2011 "informed by" a Draft Protocol on Cluster Munitions. However, the CCW states-parties were unable to reach agreement on a protocol during their November 2011 review conference.

---

[90] The White House Office of the Press Secretary, "Statement by NSC Spokesperson Caitlin Hayden on U.S. Anti-Personnel Landmine Policy," June 27, 2014.

[91] Rick Gladstone, "U.S. Chided for Delays Over Treaty on Weapons," *New York Times*, June 25, 2014.

[92] For detailed information, see CRS Report RS22907, *Cluster Munitions: Background and Issues for Congress*, by Andrew Feickert and Paul K. Kerr.

[93] Information in this section is from an Arms Control Association Fact Sheet. "Convention on Certain Conventional Weapons Convention (CCW) at a Glance," Washington, DC, October 2007.

[94] Report from the November 2007 meeting of states-parties to the CCW, December 3, 2007. http://www.unog.ch/80256EDD006B8954/(httpAssets)/029247C7A309EAC2C12573CF005B93B6/$file/CCW+MSP+2007+5+E.pdf.

Convention on Cluster Munitions (CCM)

A number of CCW members, led by Norway, initiated negotiations in 2007 outside of the CCW to ban cluster munitions.[95] On May 30, 2008, they reached an agreement to ban cluster munitions.[96] The United States, Russia, China, Israel, Egypt, India, and Pakistan did not participate in the talks or sign the agreement. During the Signing Conference in Oslo from December 3-4, 2008, 94 states signed the convention and 4 of the signatories ratified the convention at the same time.[97] China, Russia, and the United States abstained, but France, Germany, and the United Kingdom were among the 18 NATO members to sign the convention.[98] As of September 14, 2013, 113 nations had signed the convention and 84 had ratified it. The convention entered into force on August 1, 2010.

The Convention on Cluster Munitions (CCM), inter alia, bans the use of cluster munitions, as well as their development, production, acquisition, transfer, and stockpiling.[99] The Convention does not prohibit cluster munitions that can detect and engage a single target or explosive submunitions equipped with an electronic self-destruction or self-deactivating feature[100]—an exemption that seemingly permits sensor-fuzed or "smart" cluster submunitions.

[95] Arms Control Association Fact Sheet. "Convention on Certain Conventional Weapons Convention (CCW) at a Glance," Washington, DC, October 2007.

[96] Kevin Sullivan and Josh White, "111 Nations, Minus the U.S., Agree to Cluster-Bomb Ban," *Washington Post,* May 29, 2008.

[97] Convention on Cluster Munitions Homepage, http://www.clusterconvention.org/.

[98] Marina Malenic, "Dozens of Nations Sign Cluster Bomb Treaty, U.S. Begins Upgrading Related Technology," *Defense Daily,* December 5, 2008.

[99] Diplomatic Conference for the Adoption of a Convention on Cluster Munitions, Convention on Cluster Munitions, Dublin, Ireland, May 30, 2008, http://www.clustermunitionsdublin.ie/documents.asp.

[100] Ibid.

Appendix A. List of Treaties and Agreements

This appendix lists a wide range of arms control treaties and agreements. The date listed in each entry indicates the year in which the negotiations were completed. In some cases, entry into force occurred in a subsequent year.

The Geneva Protocol, 1925: Bans the use of poison gas and bacteriological weapons in warfare.

The Antarctic Treaty, 1959: Demilitarizes the Antarctic continent and provides for scientific cooperation on Antarctica.

Memorandum of Understanding ... Regarding the Establishment of a Direct Communications Link (The Hot Line Agreement), 1963: Provides for a secure, reliable communications link between Washington and Moscow. Modified in 1971, 1984, and 1988 to improve the method of communications.

Limited Test Ban Treaty, 1963: Bans nuclear weapons tests or any nuclear explosions in the atmosphere, outer space, and under water.

Outer Space Treaty, 1967: Bans the orbiting or stationing on celestial bodies (including the moon) of nuclear weapons or other weapons of mass destruction.

Treaty for the Prohibition of Nuclear Weapons in Latin America (Treaty of Tlatelolco), 1967: Obligates nations in Latin America not to acquire, possess, or store nuclear weapons on their territory.

Treaty on the Non-Proliferation of Nuclear Weapons, 1968: Non-nuclear signatories agree not to acquire nuclear weapons; nuclear signatories agree to cooperate with non-nuclear signatories in peaceful uses of nuclear energy.

Seabed Arms Control Treaty, 1971: Bans emplacement of military installations, including those capable of launching weapons, on the seabed.

Agreement on Measures to Reduce the Risk of Outbreak of Nuclear War (Accident Measures Agreement), 1971: Outlines measures designed to reduce the risk that technical malfunction, human failure, misinterpreted incident, or unauthorized action could start a nuclear exchange.

Biological Weapons Convention, 1972: Bans the development, production, stockpile, or acquisition of biological agents or toxins for warfare.

Agreement ... on the Prevention of Incidents On and Over the High Seas, 1972: Establishes "rules of the road" to reduce the risk that accident, miscalculation, or failure of communication could escalate into a conflict at sea.

Interim Agreement ... on Certain Measures with Respect to the Limitation of Strategic Offensive Arms (SALT I Interim Agreement), 1972: Limits numbers of some types of U.S. and Soviet strategic offensive nuclear weapons.

Treaty ... on the Limitation of Anti-Ballistic Missile Systems (ABM Treaty), 1972: Limits United States and Soviet Union to two ABM sites each; limits the number of interceptor missiles and radars at each site to preclude nationwide defense. Modified in 1974 to permit one ABM site in each nation. U.S. withdrew in June 2002.

Agreement ... on the Prevention of Nuclear War, 1973: United States and Soviet Union agreed to adopt an "attitude of international cooperation" to prevent the development of situations that might lead to nuclear war.

Treaty ... on the Limitation of Underground Nuclear Weapons Tests (Threshold Test Ban Treaty), 1974: Prohibits nuclear weapons tests with yields of more than 150 kilotons. Ratified and entered into force in 1990.

Treaty ... on Underground Nuclear Explosions for Peaceful Purposes (Peaceful Nuclear Explosions Treaty), 1976: Extends the limit of 150 kilotons to nuclear explosions occurring outside weapons test sites. Ratified and entered into force in 1990.

Concluding Document of the Conference on Security and Cooperation in Europe (Helsinki Final Act), 1975: Outlines notifications and confidence-building measures with respect to military activities in Europe.

Convention on the Prohibition of Military or any other Hostile Use of Environmental Modification Techniques, 1978: Bans the hostile use of environmental modification techniques that have lasting or widespread effects.

Treaty ... on the Limitation of Strategic Offensive Arms (SALT II), 1979: Places quantitative and qualitative limits on some types of U.S. and Soviet strategic offensive nuclear weapons. Never ratified.

The Convention on Prohibitions or Restrictions on the Use of Certain Conventional Weapons Which May Be Deemed To Be Excessively Injurious or To Have Indiscriminate Effects: This Convention, also known as the Convention on Conventional Weapons (CCW), was concluded in Geneva in 1980 and entered into force in 1993. Protocol II (Protocol on Prohibitions or Restrictions on the Use of Mines, Booby-traps and Other Devices) contains rules for marking, registering, and removing minefields, in an effort to reduce indiscriminate casualties caused by anti-personnel landmines. Protocol IV prohibits laser weapons designed to cause blindness.

Document of the Stockholm Conference on Confidence- and Security-Building Measures and Disarmament in Europe (Stockholm Document), 1986: Expands on the notifications and confidence-building measures in the Helsinki Final Act. Provides for ground and aerial inspection of military activities.

Treaty of Rarotonga, 1986: Establishes a Nuclear Weapons Free Zone in the South Pacific. The United States signed the Protocols in 1996; the Senate has not yet provided its advice and consent to ratification.

Agreement ... on the Establishment of Nuclear Risk Reduction Centers, 1987: Establishes communications centers in Washington and Moscow and improves communications links between the two.

Treaty ... on the Elimination of their Intermediate-Range and Shorter-Range Missiles, 1987: Bans all U.S. and Soviet ground-launched ballistic and cruise missiles with ranges between 300 and 3,400 miles.

Agreement ... on Notifications of Launches of Intercontinental Ballistic Missiles and Submarine Launched Ballistic Missiles, 1988: Obligates United States and Soviet Union to provide at least 24 hours' notice before the launch of an ICBM or SLBM.

Agreement on the Prevention of Dangerous Military Activities, 1989: Outlines cooperative procedures that are designed to prevent and resolve peacetime incidents between the armed forces of the United States and Soviet Union.

U.S.-U.S.S.R. Chemical Weapons Destruction Agreement, 1990: Mandates the destruction of the bulk of the U.S. and Soviet chemical weapons stockpiles.

Vienna Document of the Negotiations on Confidence- and Security-Building Measures, 1990: Expands on the measures in the 1986 Stockholm Document.

Treaty on Conventional Armed Forces in Europe (CFE Treaty), 1990: Limits and reduces the numbers of certain types of conventional armaments deployed from the "Atlantic to the Urals."

Treaty ... on the Reduction and Limitation of Strategic Offensive Arms (START), 1991: Limits and reduces the numbers of strategic offensive nuclear weapons. Modified by the Lisbon Protocol of 1992 to provide for Belarus, Ukraine, Kazakhstan, and Russia to succeed to Soviet Union's obligations under the Treaty. Entered into force on December 5, 1994.

Vienna Document of the Negotiations on Confidence- and Security-Building Measures, 1992: Expands on the measures in the 1990 Vienna Document.

Treaty on Open Skies, 1992: Provides for overflights by unarmed observation aircraft to build confidence and increase transparency of military activities.

Agreement ... Concerning the Safe and Secure Transportation, Storage, and Destruction of Weapons and Prevention of Weapons Proliferation, 1992: Provides for U.S. assistance to Russia for the safe and secure transportation, storage, and destruction of nuclear, chemical, and other weapons.

Agreement Between the United States and Republic of Belarus Concerning Emergency Response and the Prevention of Proliferation of Weapons of Mass Destruction, 1992: Provides for U.S. assistance to Belarus in eliminating nuclear weapons and responding to nuclear emergencies in Belarus.

Treaty ... on the Further Reduction and Limitation of Strategic Offensive Arms (START II) 1993: Would have further reduced the number of U.S. and Russian strategic offensive nuclear weapons. Would have banned the deployment of all land-based multiple-warhead missiles (MIRVed ICBMs), including the Soviet SS-18 "heavy" ICBM. Signed on January 3, 1993; U.S. Senate consented to ratification in January 1996; Russian Duma approved ratification in April 2000. Treaty never entered into force.

Convention on the Prohibition of the Development, Production, Stockpiling and Use of Chemical Weapons and on their Destruction: Bans chemical weapons and requires elimination of their production facilities. Opened for signature on January 13, 1993; entered into force in April 1997.

Agreement ... Concerning the Disposition of Highly Enriched Uranium Resulting from the Dismantlement of Nuclear Weapons in Russia, 1993: Provides for U.S. purchase of highly enriched uranium removed from Russian nuclear weapons; uranium to be blended into low enriched uranium for fuel in commercial nuclear reactors. Signed and entered into force on February 18, 1993.

Agreement Between the United States and Ukraine Concerning Assistance to Ukraine in the Elimination of Strategic Nuclear Arms, and the Prevention of Proliferation of Weapons of Mass Destruction: Provides for U.S. assistance to Ukraine to eliminate nuclear weapons and implement provisions of START I. Signed in late 1993, entered into force in 1994.

Agreement Between the United States and Republic of Kazakhstan Concerning the Destruction of Silo Launchers of Intercontinental Ballistic Missiles, Emergency Response, and the Prevention of Proliferation of Weapons of Mass Destruction, 1993: Provides for U.S. assistance to Kazakhstan to eliminate nuclear weapons and implement provisions of START I.

Trilateral Statement by the Presidents of the United States, Russia, and Ukraine, 1994: Statement in which Ukraine agreed to transfer all nuclear warheads on its territory to Russia in exchange for security assurances and financial compensation. Some compensation will be in the form of fuel for Ukraine's nuclear reactors. The United States will help finance the compensation by purchasing low enriched uranium derived from dismantled weapons from Russia.

Treaty of Pelindaba, 1996: Establishes a nuclear weapons free zone in Africa. The United States has signed, but not yet ratified Protocols to the Treaty.

Comprehensive Nuclear Test Ban Treaty (CTBT), 1996: Bans all nuclear explosions, for any purpose. The United States and more than 130 other nations had signed the Treaty by late 1996. The U.S. Senate voted against ratification in October, 1999.

Ottawa Treaty, 1997: Convention for universal ban against the use of anti-personnel landmines, signed in 1997 and entered into force in 1999. The United States and other significant military powers are not signatories.

Strategic Offensive Reductions Treaty (Moscow Treaty), 2002: Obligates the United States and Russia to reduce strategic nuclear forces to between 1,700 and 2,200 warheads. Does not define weapons to be reduced or provide monitoring and verification provisions. Reductions must be completed by December 31, 2012. Treaty lapsed upon entry into force of New START. Signed in May 2002, entered into force June 1, 2003.

Treaty ... On Measures for the Further Reduction and Limitation of Strategic Offensive Arms (New START), 2010: Obligates the United States and Russia to reduce strategic nuclear forces to 1,550 warheads on up to 700 deployed delivery vehicles, within a total of 800 deployed and nondeployed delivery vehicles. Reductions must occur within 7 years, treaty remains in force for 10 years. Signed on April 10, 2010, entered into force on February 5, 2011.

Appendix B. The U.S. Treaty Ratification Process

Article II, Section 2, Clause 2 of the U.S. Constitution establishes responsibilities for treaty ratification. It provides that the President "shall have Power, by and with the Advice and Consent of the Senate, to make Treaties, provided two thirds of the Senators present concur." Contrary to common perceptions, the Senate does not ratify treaties; it provides its advice and consent to ratification by passing a resolution of ratification. The President then "ratifies" a treaty by signing the instrument of ratification and either exchanging it with the other parties to the treaty or depositing it at a central repository (such as the United Nations).

In Section 33 of the Arms Control and Disarmament Act (P.L. 87-297, as amended), Congress outlined the relationship between arms control agreements and the treaty ratification process. This law provides that "no action shall be taken under this or any other law that will obligate the United States to disarm or to reduce or to limit the Armed Forces or armaments of the United States, except pursuant to the treaty-making power of the President under the Constitution or unless authorized by further affirmative legislation by the Congress of the United States."

In practice, most U.S. arms control agreements have been submitted as treaties, a word reserved in U.S. usage for international agreements submitted to the Senate for its approval in accordance with Article II, Section 2 of the Constitution. The Senate clearly expects future arms control obligations would be made only pursuant to treaty in one of its declarations in the resolution of ratification of the START Treaty. The declaration stated: "The Senate declares its intention to consider for approval international agreements that would obligate the United States to reduce or limit the Armed Forces or armaments of the United States in a militarily significant manner only pursuant to the treaty power set forth in Article II, Section 2, Clause 2 of the Constitution."

Nonetheless, some arms control agreements have been made by other means. Several "confidence building" measures have been concluded as legally binding international agreements, called executive agreements in the United States, without approval by Congress. These include the Hot Line Agreement of June 20, 1963, the Agreement on Prevention of Nuclear War of June 22, 1973, and agreements concluded in the Standing Consultative Commission established by the Anti-ballistic Missile Treaty. In another category that might be called statutory or congressional-executive agreements, the SALT I Interim Agreement was approved by a joint resolution of Congress in 1972. In a third category, the executive branch has entered some arms control agreements that it did not submit to Congress on grounds that they were "politically binding" but not "legally binding." Such agreements include several measures agreed to through the Conference on Security and Cooperation in Europe, such as the Stockholm Document on Confidence- and Security-Building Measures and Disarmament in Europe, signed September 19, 1986.

Senate Consideration

The conclusion or signing of a treaty is only the first step toward making the agreement legally binding on the parties. First, the parties decide whether to ratify, that is, express their consent to be bound by, the treaty that the negotiators have signed. Each party follows its own constitutional process to approve the treaty.

In the United States, after a treaty has been signed, the President at a time of his choice submits to the Senate the treaty and any documents that are to be considered an integral part of the treaty and requests the Senate's advice and consent to ratification. The President's message is accompanied by a letter from the Secretary of State to the President which contains an analysis of the treaty. After submittal, the Senate may approve the agreement, approve it with various conditions, or not approve it.

Senate consideration of a treaty is governed by Senate Rule XXX, which was amended in 1986 to simplify the procedure.[101] The treaty is read a first time and the injunction of secrecy is removed by unanimous consent, although normally the text of a treaty has already been made public. The treaty is then referred to the Senate Committee on Foreign Relations under Senate Rule XXV on jurisdiction. After consideration, the committee reports the treaty to the Senate with a proposed resolution of ratification that may contain any of the conditions described below. If the committee objects to a treaty, or believes the treaty would not receive the necessary majority in the Senate, it usually simply does not report the treaty to the Senate and the treaty remains pending indefinitely on the committee calendar.[102]

After it is reported from the committee, a treaty is required to lie over for one calendar day before Senate consideration. The Senate considers the treaty after adoption of a non-debatable motion to go into executive session for that purpose.[103] Rule XXX provides that the treaty then be read a second time, after which amendments to the treaty may be proposed. The majority leader typically asks unanimous consent that the treaty be considered to have passed through all the parliamentary stages up to and including the presentation of the resolution of ratification. After the resolution of ratification is presented, amendments to the treaty itself, which are rare, may not be proposed. The resolution of ratification is then "open to amendment in the form of reservations, declarations, statements, or understandings." Decisions on amendments and conditions are made by a majority vote. Final approval of the resolution of ratification with any conditions that have been approved, requires a two-thirds majority of those Senators present.

After approving the treaty, the Senate returns it to the President with the resolution of ratification. If he accepts the conditions of the Senate, the President then ratifies the treaty by signing a document referred to as an instrument of ratification. Included in the instrument of ratification are any of the Senate conditions that State Department officials consider require tacit or explicit approval by the other party. The ratification is then complete at the national level and ready for exchange or deposit. The treaty enters into force in the case of a bilateral treaty upon exchange of instruments of ratification and in the case of a multilateral treaty with the deposit of the number of ratifications specified in the treaty. The President then signs a document called a proclamation which publicizes the treaty domestically as in force and the law of the land.

If the President objects to any of the Senate conditions, or if the other party to a treaty objects to any of the conditions and further negotiations occur, the President may resubmit the treaty to the Senate for further consideration or simply not ratify it.

---

[101] The 1986 amendment eliminated a stage in which the Senate met "as in Committee of the Whole" and acted on any proposed amendment to the treaty.

[102] For further information, see *Rejection of Treaties: A Brief Survey of Past Instances.* CRS Report No. 87-305 F, by Ellen C. Collier, March 30, 1987. (Archived. For copies, call Amy Woolf, 202-707-2379.)

[103] Earlier, treaties could only be taken out of the order in which they were reported from the committee and appeared on the Senate Executive Calendar by debatable motion. In 1977 the Threshold Test Ban and Peaceful Nuclear Explosions Treaties were ordered reported by the committee and then delayed partly so that they would not be placed on the Senate calendar ahead of the Panama Canal Treaties. Senate Committee on Foreign Relations. *Treaties and Other International Agreements: The Role of the United States Senate.* November 1993, p. 101.

Approval with Conditions

The Senate may stipulate various conditions on its approval of a treaty. Major types of Senate conditions include amendments, reservations, understandings, and declarations or other statements or provisos. Sometimes the executive branch recommends the conditions, such as the December 16, 1974, reservation to the 1925 Geneva Protocol prohibiting the use of poison gas and the understandings on the protocols to the Treaty for the Prohibition of Nuclear Weapons in Latin America.

An amendment to a treaty proposes a change to the language of the treaty itself, and Senate adoption of amendments to the text of a treaty is infrequent. A formal amendment to a treaty after it has entered into force is made through an additional treaty often called a protocol. An example is the ABM (Anti-Ballistic Missile) Protocol, signed July 3, 1974, which limited the United States and the Soviet Union to one ABM site each instead of two as in the original 1972 ABM Treaty. While the Senate did not formally attach amendments to the 1974 Threshold Test Ban and 1976 Peaceful Nuclear Explosion treaties, it was not until Protocols relating to verification were concluded in 1990 that the Senate approved these two Treaties.

A reservation is a limitation or qualification that changes the obligations of one or more of the parties. A reservation must be communicated to the other parties and, in a bilateral treaty, explicitly agreed to by the other party. President Nixon requested a reservation to the Geneva Protocol on the use of poison gases stating that the protocol would cease to be binding on the United States in regard to an enemy state if that state or any of its allies failed to respect the prohibition. One of the conditions attached to the INF treaty might be considered a reservation although it was not called that. On the floor the sponsors referred to it as a Category III condition. The condition was that the President obtain Soviet consent that a U.S.-Soviet agreement concluded on May 12, 1988, be of the same effect as the provisions of the treaty.

An understanding is an interpretation or elaboration ordinarily considered consistent with the treaty. In 1980, the Senate added five understandings to the agreement with the International Atomic Energy Agency (IAEA) for the Application of Safeguards in the United States. The understandings concerned implementation of the agreement within the United States. A condition added to the INF treaty resolution, requiring a presidential certification of a common understanding on ground-launched ballistic missiles, might be considered an understanding. The sponsor of the condition, Senator Robert Dole, said, "this condition requires absolutely nothing more from the Soviets, but it does require something from our President."[104]

A declaration states policy or positions related to the treaty but not necessarily affecting its provisions. Frequently, like some of the understandings mentioned above, declarations and other statements concern internal procedures of the United States rather than international obligations and are intended to assure that Congress or the Senate participate in subsequent policy. The resolution of ratification of the Threshold Test Ban Treaty adopted in 1990 made approval subject to declarations (1) that to preserve a viable deterrent a series of specified safeguards should be an ingredient in decisions on national security programs and the allocation of resources, and (2) the United States shared a special responsibility with the Soviet Union to continue talks seeking a verifiable comprehensive test ban. In a somewhat different step, in 1963 the Senate attached a preamble to the resolution of ratification of the limited nuclear test ban treaty. The preamble

---

[104] *Congressional Record*, May 27, 1988, p. S 6883.

contained three "Whereas" clauses of which the core one stated that amendments to treaties are subject to the constitutional process.

The important distinction among the various conditions concerns their content or effect. Whatever designation the Senate applies to a condition, if the President determines that it may alter an international obligation under the treaty, he transmits it to the other party or parties and further negotiations or abandonment of the treaty may result.

During its consideration of the SALT II Treaty, the Senate Foreign Relations Committee grouped conditions into three categories to clarify their intended legal effect; (I) those that need not be formally communicated to or agreed to by the Soviet Union, (II) those that would be formally communicated to the Soviet Union, but not necessarily agreed to by them, and (III) those that would require the explicit agreement of the Soviet Union. In the resolution of ratification of the START Treaty, the Senate made explicit that some of the conditions were to be communicated to the other parties.

The Senate approves most treaties without formally attaching conditions. Ten arms control treaties were adopted without conditions: the Antarctic, Outer Space, Nuclear Non-Proliferation, Seabed, ABM, Environmental Modification, and Peaceful Nuclear Explosions Treaties, the Biological Weapons and the Nuclear Materials Conventions, and the ABM Protocol. In some of these cases, however, the Senate Foreign Relations Committee included significant understandings in its report.

Even when it does not place formal conditions in the resolution of ratification, the Senate may make its views known or establish requirements on the executive branch in the report of the Foreign Relations Committee or through other vehicles.[105] Such statements become part of the legislative history but are not formally transmitted to other parties. In considering the Limited Nuclear Test Ban Treaty in 1963, the Senate turned down a reservation that "the treaty does not inhibit the use of nuclear weapons in armed conflict," but Senate leaders insisted upon a written assurance on this issue, among others, from President Kennedy. In reporting the Nuclear Non-Proliferation Treaty, the committee stated that its support of the Treaty was not to be construed as approving security assurances given to the non-nuclear-weapon parties by a U.N. Security Council resolution and declarations by the United States, the Soviet Union, and the United Kingdom. The security assurances resolution and declarations were, the committee reported, "solely executive measures."[106]

---

[105] For a discussion of methods by which Congress influences arms control negotiations, see House Committee on Foreign Affairs. *Fundamentals of Nuclear Arms Control*. Part IX—The Congressional Role in Nuclear Arms Control. Prepared for the Subcommittee on Arms Control, International Security, and Science by the Congressional Research Service. June 1986.
[106] Senate. Executive Report 91-1, March 6, 1969. 91st Congress, 1st session.

For Further Reading

The Congressional Role in Arms Control. Part IX in *Fundamentals of Nuclear Arms Control*, Subcommittee on Arms Control, International Security and Science of Committee on Foreign Affairs Committee Print, December 1986.

CRS Report No. 90-548 F, Executive Agreements Submitted to Congress: Legislative Procedures Used Since 1970. (Out of print. For copies contact Amy Woolf, 7-2379.)

CRS Report No. 93-276 F, Senate Approval of Treaties: A Brief Description with Examples from Arms Control. (Out of print. For copies contact Amy Woolf, 7-2379.)

Treaties and Other International Agreements: The Role of the United States Senate, Senate Foreign Relations Committee Print, November 1993.

Appendix C. Arms Control Organizations

Bilateral (U.S.-Former Soviet Republics)	Jurisdiction	Mandate and issues currently under discussion
Standing Consultative Commission (SCC)	ABM Treaty	Established to resolve compliance questions and to consider amendments to Treaty; currently debating ABM/TMD demarcation issues—no longer operating
Special Verification Commission (SVC)	INF Treaty	Established to resolve compliance questions; continues to discuss issues raised during monitoring and inspection process—no longer operating
Joint Compliance and Inspection Commission (JCIC)	START I	Established to resolve compliance questions and to promote implementation; meetings began before Treaty was ratified
Delegation on Safety, Security and Disarmament of Nuclear Weapons (SSD)	Nunn-Lugar Cooperative Threat Reduction Programs	U.S. delegations meet with counterparts in former Soviet republics to identify areas where U.S. assistance is needed and to implement programs
Bilateral Consultative Commission	New START Treaty	U.S. and Russian delegations meet to promote the objectives and implementation of the provisions the Treaty
Multilateral		
Conference on Disarmament (CD)	Multilateral negotiations under the U.N.	Negotiating Fissile Material Production Ban and ban on the export of anti-personnel landmines
Joint Consultative Group (JCG)	CFE Treaty	Established to resolve compliance questions and to ease implementation; recent discussions have addressed Russian request for changes in some Treaty limits
Open Skies Consultative Committee (OSCC)	Open Skies Treaty	Established to facilitate implementation of the Treaty; it has already addressed a number of technical, procedural and cost issues related to Open Skies flights
Organization for the Prohibition of Chemical Weapons (OPCW)	Chemical Weapons Convention	Established to oversee CWC implementation and monitor chemical industry worldwide; preparatory commission is currently working out the procedural details for OPCW
Comprehensive Nuclear Test-Ban Treaty Organization	Comprehensive Nuclear Test Ban Treaty	Oversees three groups—a Conference of States Parties, an Executive Council, and a Technical Secretariat—responsible for implementing the CTBT

Author Contact Information

Amy F. Woolf
Specialist in Nuclear Weapons Policy
awoolf@crs.loc.gov, 7-2379

Mary Beth D. Nikitin
Specialist in Nonproliferation
mnikitin@crs.loc.gov, 7-7745

Paul K. Kerr
Analyst in Nonproliferation
pkerr@crs.loc.gov, 7-8693

Acknowledgments

The authors would like to thank Casper Oswald for his assistance in preparing the entry on the Arms Trade Treaty.

www.ingramcontent.com/pod-product-compliance
Lightning Source LLC
Chambersburg PA
CBHW080520290526
45790CB00006B/2249